Rebellious *Daughter*

AMELIA ROSE

authorHOUSE

AuthorHouse™
1663 Liberty Drive
Bloomington, IN 47403
www.authorhouse.com
Phone: 1 (800) 839-8640

Published by AuthorHouse   05/08/2018

ISBN: 978-1-5462-3102-8 (sc)
ISBN: 978-1-5462-3100-4 (hc)
ISBN: 978-1-5462-3101-1 (e)

Library of Congress Control Number: 2018902480

Print information available on the last page.

This book is printed on acid-free paper.

Scripture quotations marked NIV are taken from the Holy Bible, New International Version®. NIV®. Copyright © 1973, 1978, 1984 by International Bible Society. Used by permission of Zondervan. All rights reserved. [Biblica]

I will never forget that last twenty-four hours when my life would change forever...

Being a single mom of two teenagers one fifteen-year-old daughter, and a sixteen-year-old son was proving to be more difficult every day the struggle was real.

What brought me to prostitution and walking out of God's will for my life? I was already working two jobs and on my own and not having the faith in what God could do. I was doing everything on my strength.

All the bills were two months behind just enough food but barely, I would skip meals to feed my kids and now that was pushing my back against a wall.

I picked up my daughter from school after work to go get groceries for supper I only had exactly $10.00 to my name, so got our food and went to pay that will be $11.40. I feel the hot flush rush to my face of fear and shame. I tell my daughter to wait there and the clerk I have change in my truck, that embarrassment was overwhelming.

To see my daughters, look of shame, it took me 10 minutes to find change in my truck literally down to the last penny.

I apologized to her and promised her things are going to get better.

Well two days later I go to work and I get pulled over, I thought I had till the end of the month to pay my insurance but nope so my truck gets impounded and I am at a complete low in my life, I need to drive my kids to school and I need to drive to work!

I had a non-Christian friend who came over for a coffee and to try and be of some encouragement she knew how desperate I was, as I was sitting there pouring my heart out to her she told me I was charming and beautiful and that men would pay to spend time with me.

She went into great detail how to do it, she had a friend who did it before.

My first thought was how can I do this???

I am a Christian it goes against everything I believed!

So, I made a deal with God, I begged and pleaded for this cup to be taken from me! I would wait for twenty-four hrs for a miracle to happen, I've heard of miracles happening all the time in my church. This was my ultimate mistake I was putting God on a timetable, being prideful not listening to reason but acting on my own desperation, not on the truth of his promises.

Lamentations 3:22-25

Because of the Lord's great love, we are not consumed, for his compassions never fail.

They are new every morning, great is your faithfulness.

I say to myself "the Lord is my portion", therefore, I will wait for Him!

Hebrews 10:23

> Let us hold on unswervingly to the hope we
> profess, for he who promised is faithful.

Proverbs 3:7-8

Be not wise in your own eyes, fear the Lord, and turn away from evil.

It will be healing to your flesh and refreshment to your bones.

I waited until the last minute and my miracle did not happen so I gave up on God. I took it upon myself to make my miracle happen, I was blinded by sin and pride. So, I posted an ad on Craigslist offering my services I would meet them in a parking lot, and we would go get business done, then he drops me off and pays me.

The number of emails was insane so I made my first appointment for that evening I still remember it was a cold November night my hands were shaking so bad I could barely drive out of fear.

I pull up and wait still believing that miracle might still happen, my phone goes off it's the man I am supposed to meet! Time has run out I start to cry but I stop myself I cannot fall apart; my family needs this money I can feel my heart harden towards God I knew I was stepping out of his blessing but desperation and fear consumed me.

I step out into the cold wind and it numbs me I get into his vehicle and we go and get business done. The shame and disgust I feel of myself I numb out, I numb God out.

Twenty-four more men I need to service to get my truck back the next couple days are a blur of work, kids and now this evening gig.

I would break down and cry after each man I felt shame, guilt, regret, the dirtiest feeling I couldn't wash off the men even after they left, it lingered on me regret was always present. But after a few times whenever I wanted to break down I would stop myself look at myself in the mirror and say don't you dare cry you are strong enough to do this.

It took me four days to make the fifteen hundred dollars I needed to get my truck back and pay for my license

One of my family members found out what I was doing and sent my ad on Facebook to my 'friends' list the next day and lost everyone in my life except my kids and one friend.

Five years later I have given up all my so-called friends, I am left with my kids my church and my mentor and my prayer warrior friend. As lonely as it is at times I have chosen to give up everything in this life to follow Christ I hustle for the gospel now.

Giving up my old lifestyle was the hardest on weekends, that's when my flesh would entice me craving all the drugs, sex, booze and attention from men. All the dancing and thrills I was missing out on. But then I would remind myself of the hangovers with the booze. The days of not sleeping from the cocaine and the dirtiest feeling I carried after random sex.

The disconnection I felt with God, not wanting to face the fact I was totally out of control when I was under the influence of all these things. When I allowed myself to be smothered in all the sin and the folly of the world, I myself snuffed out God.

I could feel my rebellious spirit come out. And I would put God on pause while I went and had my fun. After sobering up and coming down off the high from drugs I would feel defeated the enemy would come in like a lion sneering wasn't it fun last night, you were able to let loose and those people are the ones that are there for you. Look at all the attention they give you.

Now I was the type of woman who was the life of the party to the extreme, if there was a party happening and it was not raging I would get a call Amelia get down here this party needs life brought into it. I would run there with a bottle of tequila in one hand, a bag of cocaine in the other. I was the type that would dance on top of the tables telling everyone around me, live in the moment you only live once! And I had the ability to turn these people around they would all hop on my party bus. I always knew I was charismatic, but I was using it for the wrong thing, I used it to bring death in people, not life.

I have had to replace all those things, and the more I did and chastised my own will in my life, the more God rewarded me the biggest blessing is the peace that filled me, the purpose I have now in my life. A feeling that I finally belong. And people in my life seeing the changes in me. My daughter was the first one to mention it. Ma you have changed so much in this past year, I beam widely thanks to Jesus my girl!!!

Then after a few months, Holy Spirit started showing me where I was being victorious, and it would usually come at a point where I was being deceived I was getting lost in my old habits again, getting tired starting to let pity slip in my mind.

The attacks from the enemy kept coming viciously and relentlessly, where it brought me to my knees, and with each hard blow God would gently guide me, calming me pulling me into his presence, then one day after having rough couple days and my rebellious spirit coming out I was in the battle over my mind. The enemy began by trying to tell me my book was a joke, no one wants to hear anything from a hooker. Ouch, and his attack on me was relentless.

I actually felt myself slipping into a place I went when I had to numb myself to get through the times I had to be with these men. I was giving all my power over to the enemy and he was gaining territory over me. The enemy Satan saw how he was affecting me I curled up in a fetus position and listened to all he had to say about me. I didn't know how to fight back, it got to the point that I was about to go to my computer which had all the work I did on it for this book and throw it off my eleventh-floor balcony. He went on saying how I was a terrible mother, and I had no worth I was a used up addict no man will ever want me after they find out what I did, He whispered look at yourself no friends no one you are all alone. Where is your God? he sneered I was down for the count. I felt like a boxer who had just got the final blow the knockout. I was going to stay down for the count.

Then when I was about to let his evil lies consume me, I was starting to say to myself well it's not too late you can go back to that life. As soon as I see myself lying in that bed again with all those men, the Holy Spirit started guiding me back into his light and love and mercy. Just be still and know I am God, I obeyed I thought about what it would cost me if I did go back. Then Jesus started to show me how far I've come how many victories I have had, how many things I was continuing to conquer.

And remind me when I get lost to come into His presence I have tried everything else in this world Jesus is what works for me. And as long as I pursue His righteousness and His glory no matter where I am no matter what mindset. Once I calm all that is around me and open up my Spirit to Holy Spirit He replaces all the lies with His truth. All the anger and doubt with love and mercy. He knows what we go through He feels all the pain we have and he is the almighty healer.

Deuteronomy 31:5-7

The Lord will deliver them to you, and you must do to them all that I have commanded of you. Be strong and courageous. Do not be afraid or terrified because of them, for the Lord your God goes with you, he will never leave or forsake you.

I want Jesus I want to be obedient and follow Him. Obedience is something I have always battled against but he is real and he is so worth the cost of that old life, I am not alone ever he is my shepherd and protector.

Chapter Two

Picking Up Your Cross

Luke 14:25

Large crowds were travelling with Jesus, and turning to them said, if anyone comes to me and does not hate his father or mother, his wife and children, his brothers and sisters and yes even his own life, he cannot become my disciple. And anyone who does not carry his cross and follow me cannot be my disciple.

Matthew 4:18-22

As Jesus was walking beside the Sea of Galilee, he saw two brothers, Simon called Peter and his brother Andrew. They were casting a net into the lake, for they were fishermen. Come follow me Jesus said, "and I will make you fishers of men. At once they left their nets and followed Him.

Going on from there, he saw two other brothers, James son of Zebedee and his brother John.

They were in a boat with their father Zebedee, preparing their nets. Jesus called them, and immediately they left the boat and their father and followed Him.

Are you willing to follow Him?

When we come to the realization that when we choose to pick up our cross and follow Him. The old us dies, we choose to stay on the path to our God-given destiny, that God has given us our own free will. Not everyone that has been on our life journey will continue, and I have mourned some of the people I had to leave behind. After inviting them to church trying to bring them to Jesus but choose to stay in the world.

Mathew 10:14

If anyone will not welcome you or listen to your message, shake its dust off your feet as you leave.

Slowly God brought to the realization what it meant to be unequally yoked the struggle to stay in God's will for your life will be much harder. And your fight will be even harder because your faith will be tested and judged even more.

2 Corinthians 6:14

Do not be yoked together with unbelievers. For what do righteousness and wickedness have in common? Or what fellowship can light have with darkness?

BOOM revelation!!! That is exactly what it was like being in relationships with men that did not believe. It was like having a candle lit and the other person dislikes the smell of it and keeps blowing it out. I had to snuff out my light to stay in the darkness to be in union with them. Holy Spirit Seeks union in Him at all times. Where there is no peace there is no unity.

Or being in friendships where you are not in a union and that doesn't encourage you or help get you to your next level with the Holy Spirit. And Jesus knows how hard and painful the process can be with having to weed out the toxic ones in your life, and like me, you might be left with only one or two good after God's own heart kind of people. I just want to encourage you that you are not alone. Ask Him to reveal to you the people you need to remove from your life and the courage and his strength to do it.

Colossians 2:2 5

I want you to know how much I am struggling for you and for those at Laodicea, and for all who have not seen me personally. My purpose is that they may be encouraged in heart and united in love, so that they may have the full riches of complete understanding, in order that they may know the mystery of God, namely Christ, in whom are hidden all the treasures of wisdom and knowledge. I tell you this so that no one may deceive you by fine-sounding arguments. For though I am absent with you in body, I am present with you in spirit and delight to see how orderly you are and how firm your faith in Christ is.

Psalm 133:1

How good and pleasant it is when brothers live together in unity. It's like precious oil being poured on the head.

Romans 15:5

May the God who gives endurance and encouragement give you a spirit of unity, among your selves as you follow Christ Jesus, so that with one heart and mouth you may glorify the God and Father of our Lord Jesus Christ.

Ephesians 4:3

As a prisoner of the Lord, then I urge you to live a life worthy of the calling you have received. Be patient, bearing with one another in love. Make every effort to keep the unity of the spirit through the bond of peace. There is only one body and one Spirit – just as you were called to one hope when you were called – one Lord, one faith, one baptism, one God, and Father of all, who is over all through all and in all.

Colossians 3:14

And over all these virtues put on love, which binds them all together in perfect unity.

God would speak to my heart I would try and share with my partner I had at that time, but it was like speaking a different language to him, and he would even say that to me. He would say it's like I speak Spanish and he speaks Japanese. Then I would have to keep all the blessings God was bestowing on me because he wouldn't celebrate them with me, almost like he was jealous of the favour I received. So, I started toning down my walk with God in front of him.

I know God is with us in all things in all situations when we choose to still seek him, he may not agree with it. But he will honour his promises to us to never leave us or forsake us.

God wants us in unity with Him and our relationships, but back then I was unconscionable I started isolating myself from the shame of what I did. I stuck with people who accepted what I did. I didn't want to have to answer any questions new people might ask like what you do for a living etc., etc. was easier just staying alone or with likeminded people that were as lost as I was.

Making a destructive choice and listening to the lies of the enemy is why I became a high-end escort, I became a Gomer. Catering to the prestige's men of my city. See they seen the Charm in me were drawn to my attention I poured on them. Manipulating them with my words and my body. They were bored in their marriage or alone and I was the one they would come too. I would need their money and devotion.

Becoming addictive to the attention they gave me, their gifts, compliments, favours and money and time. Again, I was putting my worth on men, but I still hand one hand on Jesus.

The story of Hosea and Gomer
Loving pursuit of the unfaithful

Hosea delivers this message of warning to the northern Kingdom of Israel just a few short years before they are sent into exile. Israel has made unwise alliances with Assyria and Egypt (Hos 7:11) and adopted their idolatrous practices. The events of Hosea's personal life parallel the sins of the people and God's unconditional love for them, as well as reminding the people of God's unconditional love for them, as well as reminding the people of God's promised judgement for disobedience.

Hosea's story is a painful tale of love and unfaithfulness. At God's command, Hosea takes Gomer as his wife. She is unfaithful to him, paralleling Israel's unfaithfulness to God.

The children born of their union are given names dictated by God.

Our hearts break when Hosea names one of his children "Lo-Ramah" meaning not loved, and another 'Lo-Ammi' meaning not my people. Yet as we follow the book to its conclusion, we also find a reason for hope. When Hosea lovingly brings Gomer home from following her descent into prostitution, God reveals his loving restoration of his people. (Hos 3). And God announces to Hosea that he will not always call his people 'not loved' and "not my people". When they turn to him, he will show them his love and restore them. (Hos 2:23)

Hosea ends his book with a series of sermons that declare God's holiness, justice and love. Though God will discipline his people for disobedience, his compassion for them will never cease.

As Hosea seeks out his unfaithful wife and brings her back home, we are assured that, like Gomer and the Israelites, we are never too far gone from God's grace. Repentance always brings restoration and blessing. (Hos 14)

I had become a Gomer enticing my idols with my sexuality, manipulation, my charm and body, my words.

Who is my Hosea? God is and I am his Gomer. Jesus paid my price when I landed up on the auction block he paid my price for me when he gave his own life on the cross. I am no longer a sex slave or a slave in anything in, Christ there is only freedom.

Hosea means salvation, Gomer means completion.

He has searched for me in every disgusting place I have put myself in and gone to places no man would want to go. It was seeing Jesus's love for me his goodness and that no matter how disobedient I became he still wanted me, I am in awe of his goodness and his relentless love for me makes me want to change my ways. I have always been an all or nothing kind of girl, and when he would search for me I would search to see if there was one sheep where I was that wanted to come home with us.

God gave me a huge heart a love for people that you may deem unsavable, filthy, lost cause. Trust me they don't need more of your judgment or condemnation. In a lot of these situations, the enemy got a foothold in lives. Maybe life has been so cruel to them that was it, they are done and the only relief is to get high or drunk. They are lost! We are told to be bold and courageous, and do everything in love, if one of the "lost causes" was a brother, your child, your wife, would you go out to find her? My heart has ached and cried for the ones I found but refuses to come home to Jesus. I have such a hard time giving up on people, but God is showing me there are millions of lost sheep, they need to come home, all I can do is introduce them to Jesus and pray for them and love them, but if no change is happening it's time to pick up your staff and find the next lost one.

I remember one day walking past a homeless woman who was badly scarred by burns. I stopped and gave her some change; her hands shook I knew she was needing a drink. I asked her how long she had been on the street? She told me about a year,

I just stood patiently and she began to share that she had two children that had died in a house fire she tried getting to them but it was too late. The amount of pain I felt for that woman I asked if I could pray for her, she nodded yes, I prayed peace and for Jesus to come into every piece of her heart so that there was no more room for guilt or shame. That she would seek him and make him Lord and Savior of her life. Amen

Luke 15

Now the tax collectors and "sinners" were all gathering around to hear him. But the Pharisees and the teachers of the law muttered. "This man welcomes sinners and eats with them.

Then Jesus told them this parable "suppose one of you has a hundred sheep and loses one of them. Does he not leave the ninety-nine in the open country and go after the lost sheep until he finds it? And when he finds it, he joyfully puts it on his shoulders and goes home. Then he calls his friends and neighbours together and says, rejoice with me, I have found my lost sheep. I tell you, in the same way, there will be more rejoicing in heaven over one sinner who repents than over ninety-nine righteous persons who do not need to repent.

I sought instant gratification only leaned on my own understanding, and he still delivered me. He brought me out of the desert of sin even though I felt like I did not deserve it or I had not earned it. I choose to live in physical, mental and spiritual prostitution it was only when I started to walk the walk and talk the talk of his word that he began moving those mountains and parting seas in my life. To be able to let go of all your trust and hand it over to something you can't touch or see takes a huge amount faith, the faith I never knew I was possible of believing. But I do to the point there is no turning back, he is the only one that makes sense. And after you stand in his presence and say here I am God have all of me, you know he is real you can feel him in your deepest parts of your soul, and then you begin to hear him.

Gomer shows us that no matter how low we get, God does not cease to love and care for us. I prayed and he answered my prayers to not get a sexually transmitted disease from my rebellion or not get killed, and keep my heart softened not to become bitter.

There is always a way back to him. He has purchased us out of slavery with the blood of his only son Jesus. The greatness of our sin or degradation is the best reason to go to him, not a reason to stay away from him, for Jesus said "It is not the healthy who need a doctor, but the sick. I have not come to call the righteous, but sinners to repentance". And I was a lost cause, but Jesus left the ninety-nine to find me over and over again.

Jesus taught us about bringing life to those stuck in sin and in bondage, not the self-righteous who are their own Hosea.

Isaiah 61:1-3

The spirit of the Sovereign Lord is with me because the Lord has anointed me to preach good news to the poor.

He has sent me to bind up the broken-hearted, to proclaim freedom for the captives and release from darkness for the prisoners, to proclaim the year of the Lord's favour and the day of vengeance of our God, to comfort all those who mourn, and provide for those who grieve in Zion.

To bestow on them a crown of beauty instead of ashes, the oil of gladness instead of mourning, and a garment of praise instead of a spirit of despair.

They will be called oaks of righteousness, a planting of the Lord for the display of his splendour.

I had also let pride to set in and fear I became self-sufficient not letting myself need of any of others. Putting up walls around me, till I was barricaded in. Allowing my body to be used over and over was taking over my self-worth. God designed us to need him and to need others in our lives. If we only give and never receive, we should not be surprised when we come to the end of our resources. Ask the Holy Spirit to soften your hearts to let him in, and others in.

I left becoming an escort the same way I came in actually worse, no richer but total confidence in God this time I will not get it wrong, I will wait on the Lord in total faith and patience and in total trust and he will provide all I need and abundantly more than I can imagine. My part in it is to not jump ship no matter how dim it may look.

It has become my passion through Christ to find all the Gomer's God's lost rebellious children out there, and to let them know God has not forsaken you. Will you allow God to step in and be your Hosea? God has so loved us we are meant to love the unlovely. I want to love people the way God loves me. So many souls stuck on the auction block, stuck in slavery. But God is coming like a mighty warrior for our brothers and sisters in Christ and we will roar with him into the battle!

But back then I was still lost in my rebellion, still not trusting him fully. So, I made the next big step in this journey I decided to rent a hotel and post on a local escort site.

I had no idea what I was doing and still prayed before I opened the door, that God would keep me safe. And bring me home to my kids that I would be a blessing to them. I kept a photo of my kids taped in my closet as I got ready for a client I kept my eyes on them it gave me the strength to endure it., I should have been keeping my eyes on Jesus.

I still loved God and felt my heart soften to him again, and I prayed he still loved me and would forgive me.

I still wore my heart on my sleeve and still had a genuine love for people even though I was living in disobedience and sin.

Now God has brought many people into my life during this time and I remember Joel Osteen preaching on this that God will never forsake us.

And he hasn't.

Guilt and shame were ruining me but now I was stuck.

I recall going to church a couple months after starting escorting, I was so hungry for his word his presence I walked in and people I recognized came and said good morning.

I could not make eye contact with them out of shame. I, after all, was the woman at the well I knew I was not living God's will in my life. But still, I yearned for him his truth and promises.

When I got to my seat God's love surrounded me feeding my thirst and when my Pastor started preaching the first thing he said was "I would rather have the drunks, drug users and prostitutes in my church then the hypocrites that judge them.

I was welcome here no shame nothing but love and forgiveness.

I still go to my church and there had been many times I wanted to talk to someone after the service to get prayer and strength for healing from the destructive choice I made of being an escort. One day God put a mentor of mine I had lost contact with on my heart. I hadn't seen or talked to her in twelve years. I contacted her and asked if she remembered me? She immediately replied yes of course! When I first started attending Springs she taught Tuesday morning woman bible study. She was the most gracious woman I had ever met. She was mature and beautiful, classy and a woman after God's own heart. She taught me the unconditional love of Jesus and the power we have as woman, mother's, sisters, wife's, daughters. How we can minister to all those around us, and do it in love, forgiveness, grace and mercy. She had a very firm way of doing this her confidence in the word was bold and she intimidated me but God knew I would need a strong woman of God with my rebellious spirit.

I was halfway done this book when I met with her, I told her my whole story the prostitution, the addictions all the sin. She enlightened me and provided additional healing through his word.

The next day she sent me an email with the link to a song that she heard and it reminded her of me....

I need you more - Kim Walker Smith

> I listened to that song and it brought healing and
> tears of joy!
> The verse that hit home to me the hardest was....
> And Lord as time goes by

> I'll be by your side
> Cause I never want to go back to my old life

It hasn't been easy nor is it going to be easy. My journey started when I finally gave it all to God. My lifestyle was consuming me with addiction and disobedience, cocaine was eating up any extra left-over money I was making so that was the first addiction to give to God. Here have it I am out of control and dying in every sense numbed out on drugs looking all around me being surrounded by lusts and in my own pleasure drowning in my flesh.

Loneliness and the need for excitement are where I falter. Through Holy Spirit, he is showing me how good he is. The world is being consumed by addiction pills, meth, crack, cocaine and huffers (inhaling substances to get high) it is like watching the walking dead in reality, they are lost and literally become soulless their main purpose is to get the next fix I was one of them.

The epidemic of addictions is the enemy at work and he is such a lying manipulative scum bag, he is the cartel of the broken and lost he roams around looking for his next prey. It's his mission to make God's children numbed out once he has us there, he thinks he gets the upper hand and gets a foothold in our lives. He has come to kill, steal and destroy. Now think about this in your own addiction whatever it may be, he comes in sneakily.

Let's say you had an injury and you were given addictive medication to ease the pain. There is his opportunity to come in, telling you the pain is so bad you need more, the more you take the more you numb out. The more you numb out the more disconnected you become with God. Before you even realize it, he convinces you that your pain is not going away you need more pills. His goal is to keep you numb, keep you dependent on the pills, not God. Then after the pills run out and the Doc won't prescribe you anymore, the enemy now has a place in your life because you've become dependent on his lie.

He will then bring people into your life that can get you your fix. And you are grateful that these people understand your pain and need for relief. But they are just as numbed out as you. You are in like-minded company, misery loves misery. Whatever the addiction it's the same scenario, he uses his same destructive lies on all of us.

Slowly I started fellowshipping with God again I prayed my eyes be open, my ears to hear his word and his will be done in my life no matter what it meant. To pull all of the deep-rooted lies I was entrapped in, to give me the strength to bear it. Thanking Him he will never give me more then I can handle

Thank you, Jesus, God was not loosening his grip on me. Learning to walk in forgiveness for myself and silence all around me, to listen to God his will be done not my own anymore. Then getting to the point where I was only able to see enough clients to just get by paying bills.

Then in total freedom from prostitution when Jesus said this life you have been living is done. I paid the price for all your sins you are bought and paid for in my blood. It's time for you to choose are you going to trust me this time? If I stayed I knew was choosing death, only then came the moment I could not emotionally, mentally, or physically do it anymore. I lost that switch I had in my mind to turn off any emotion I had to these men. I use to be able to tap out when I was with them, I was once a great actress but now I was there with them I couldn't escape.

The last client I ever saw I knew the door was closed, I kept praying the whole time Lord let him hurry and be fast, but it ended up being the longest session I ever had, I was about to tell him to leave I started to cry I screamed in my mind no more! I yearned to have my body back ownership of my body back. And to hand over to Jesus every ounce of me all of it to his glory I will only be used again for Him.

And that is exactly what it did I stepped out in faith!

I have come to believe everything happens for a reason and its God's timing, not ours. And if we will just keep in faith and be patient, courageous in all things God will come through! I also at one time in my life took offence to anything that anybody said to me, I would go home pick apart the whole conversation, find offence "seek and you shall find" lol, imagining what my comeback should have been, how I would be the witty one next time. Then God started showing me all the anxiety I was creating for myself.

Proverbs 19:11

A man's wisdom gives him patience, it is to his glory to overlook an offence.

Colossians 1:10-14

And we pray this in order that you may live life worthy, of the Lord and may please him in every way, bearing fruit in every good work, growing in knowledge of God, being strengthened with all power according to his glorious might so that you may have great endurance and patience, and joyfully giving thanks to all the Father, who has qualified you to share in the inheritance of the saints in the kingdom of light.

For he has rescued us from the dominion of darkness and brought us into the kingdom of the Son he loves, in whom we have redemption, the forgiveness of sins.

I have also come to know as truth that it is our flesh that wants instant gratification, to ease the uncomfortable feelings we all have to deal with at times. This is the works and enticements of the enemy, emotions are our downfall at times, Holy Spirit is our intuition. When we have hurt that has not been healed, an offence we are holding on too, those things we refuse to bring out into the light for the mighty healer to heal. Those transgressions will take root and like bad weeds in a bountiful garden, it will overtake all the good. Till all that is left is not worth harvesting, the weeds snuff out all the nutrients all the produce.

It is learning to be aware the enemy will put constant lies in our minds. I was stuck in fear of so many things, being overtaken by the fear of the enemy Satan. My Pastor enlightened me when he explained to me, the devil has no power over our thoughts, he can only bombard our minds with his filth and lies. He sees how we are reacting by seeing how we react to his arrows of defeat, when he tells us that we deserve a little break from reality, a little cocaine will help that with seventeen shots of tequila…. or this will be our lucky night at the Casino, meanwhile he has been telling you that same lie for over a year now and you have lost everything waiting for that big win.

Having those one-night stands on tinder and other dating sites … you believing the lie that it's harmless. But it does bring harm living in lust, I was emerged in that lie. Looking for any affection I could get from anyone. But was always left feeling empty and dirty then I listened to the lie that if I was just giving it away I might as well get paid well for it.

Even though I was walking in sin I still had all the principles my church taught me, I still believed them and still practiced it. God will use us for his glory if we allow Him no matter where we are.

When I choose to become an escort, I wanted to do it with as much integrity and treat people with kindness and love, not get bitter and cold-hearted from it all. I choose to not judge these men brought into my life. At the same time, I was letting myself get jaded by seeing men live in such lust and sin and I would continually pray for God to not harden my heart and become bitter. But I was so stuck and so beaten down and discouraged, was walking around with my head down defeated. Clothed in shame and regret.

But God kept that flicker of light shining and that would keep me barely holding on to Jesus. And he would give me glimpses of my future pure and cleanse in his blood.

As woman, we are hard on ourselves our body image constantly comparing ourselves to one another.

I was always ashamed of my body I was at my heaviest at 300 pounds I hid behind all that flesh no one noticed me and definitely not for my body.

I shed all my extra weight a year before my separation from my ex-husband but turned to alcohol and drugs for my escape when life kicked me down to my knees and needed to tap out. I replaced the addiction of food to other things of the world.

Ashamed and broken I would ask God to forgive me to help me stay clean, but deep down I didn't want these things to go because that was my only coping vice, I still wasn't trusting God to deliver me.

I have to die to my flesh daily sometimes hourly because the old rebellious daughter wants to poke her ugly head out. Get me back off the path God has planned and assigned to me.

Chapter Three

Breaking Strongholds

The stronghold I am working through is loneliness being an escort showed me all God's children deal with this, many pay for companionship. There is only one true companion and he is ready and waiting to show you all the love, and comfort you will ever need. Will you trust Him? Ask Holy Spirit to show you his endless love for you!

How are we coping with it is where the freedom comes! I have always sought people especially men to get my comfort from my worth from, men who were just as broken as I was two equals don't make a right. The only thing I had in common with them was sin period.

I was on my way out the other day, as I opened the door a woman grabbed it. As she grabbed her Safeway bag full of what looked like her clothes, we locked eyes all I could see was anger, torment and total lost over any control she had over her emotions. I am assuming she was locked out of some type of relationship she was in. I saw myself in her feeling the abandonment she felt. I was her at one time losing all control over my own emotions of staying in a situation you know deep down in your heart is not God's will for our lives. Giving my power to people who were not worthy of it, who would use it to their own advantage.

The crying the desperation and loneliness needed to stop for these men I am leaving my desperation at the cross.

I like many of you have an addictive personality, I have heard the term before but really didn't understand what exactly that meant except I was weak-willed.

After researching it this is what I have found…

What society thinks about addiction, people that face this issue are currently defined to have a "brain disease" as promoted by the National Institute on Drug Abuse and other authorities. People who experience addictive personalities typically act on impulses and cannot deal with delayed gratification. At the same time, people with this type of personality tend to believe that they do not fit into societal norms and therefore, acting on impulses, deviate conformity to rebel. People with addictive personalities are very sensitive to emotional stress.

They have trouble handling situations that they deem frustrating, even if the event is for a short duration. The combination of low self-esteem, impulsivity and low tolerance for stress causes these individuals to have frequent mood swings and often suffer from some sort of depression. A coping mechanism to deal with their conflicting personality becomes their addiction and the addiction acts as something that the person can control when they find it difficult to control their personality traits.

People with addictive personalities typically switch from one addiction to the next. Addictive individuals feel highly insecure when it comes to relationships. they may often find it difficult to make commitments in relationships or trust their beloved because of the difficulty they find in achieving long-term goals. They constantly seek approval from others and as a result, these misunderstandings may contribute to the destruction of relationships. People suffering from addictive personality disorder usually undergo depression and anxiety, managing their emotions by developing an addiction to alcohol, other types of drugs, or pleasurable activities.

I know with my own addictions I am trying to escape the emotional pain I feel I can't deal with. The need to tap out the loneliness the boredom the unsettling feeling I get when I need to get into communion with God instead of the flesh.

What does scripture say about addiction?

John 16:33

I have told you these things, so that in me you may have peace. In this world, you will have trouble. But take heart! I have overcome the world!

James 4:7-11

Submit yourselves, then, to God. Resist the devil, and he will flee from you. Come near to God and he will come near to you. Wash your hands, you sinners, and purify your hearts, you double-minded. Grieve, mourn and wail. Change your laughter to mourning and your joy to gloom. Humble yourselves before the Lord, and he will lift you up.

1 Peter 3:11

He must turn from evil and do good, he must seek peace and pursue it

I find that flicker of light it shows me this life God has planned for me to help woman and men with the same strongholds that need to be cut down and cast out. I fight to conquer my fears all my insecurities all my addictions I leave them at the feet of Jesus.

The darkness is tormenting at times and it takes everything in me to not get consumed by it. There are only two options here to stay in the lies and darkness or rise above it. I put on worship music on I surround myself with pastor's teachings online and allow them to encourage me and lift me back up, put my fight back into me.

To get still with God so I can quiet all the lies and attacks from the enemy. It's very easy to forget how awful and tormenting it is when we lose our faith until our faith is all we are left with. When I was at my lowest and felt so alone it was hard to stay in faith that is when my rebellious spirit would rise to try and snare me keeping me down and broken.

Sometimes God will allow the fire just so other people will see he is God. He will use you as an example. They may not believe before, but when they see God show out in your life.

When they see you beat cancer, break the addiction set a new standard.

Go where you never dream, they won't be able to deny the blessing of God in your life.

Joel Osteen

Dying to self and the rebellion in me is something I have dealt with my whole life, yes, I would cry out I give you my life Lord. But I would hold on to some of the old flesh the drugs, booze and sex, men, acceptance from people, always living one foot in the grave and one foot in the world.

Letting go of the familiar and letting God, is such a journey you have to see that HE is worth it, YOU are worth it. You can't even begin to know what amazing things he has in store for you but you can have faith because he promises us that. And I know that I have been disappointed in people's empty promises. But God's promises are real, ask Holy Spirit to reveal them to you that you may stay in faith.

Think on all the blessings you are missing out on staying in denial and drowning in your flesh.

Just when I think that's it this time, I can't do any of this, the Lord whispers who I am in Christ

> I am the daughter of the highest
> I am a conqueror
> I am a victor
> I am his servant
> I am here for a purpose bigger than I can imagine ...

When I am ashamed to write about these things I have done in my disobedient life. God pushes me encourages me tells me I am making you strong, there will be haters and judgment but there is raw truth and healing in your words and my children need to hear it. For every two people who judge you, I your God will replace them with a dozen that will show you mercy.

So, I come back and pour my heart out on these pages and each page comes healing I was made for a purpose so much bigger than me or anything I can do on my own strength it pushes me on. To help others stuck in bondage and torment trust me if I can do this you can too!

Being an escort forced me to be completely raw and unhinged. I would try to hide my flaws but in having to present myself naked before these men really made me have to at least be confident in myself. I found out through a client there was a review and recommendation board for escorts. He informed me I got a review he said now that is just his opinion my heart dropped. I went and read a review a man had given me saying I was flabby, a three in looks but my attitude made up for it. I was horrified again was in a position where I gave my worth to another man who did not deserve it. I had more reviews and when I got good ones these men would band against me and accuse me of a shilling (lying write my own review)

I wanted to give up shame and embarrassment overtook me my self-esteem was so bad that I would tell a new client when he arrived that if he was disappointed in me I understood and they could leave. Having to share my body unwillingly is by far the hardest thing I have had to overcome, the feeling of wanting to scream at them to get off me but having to keep the screams inside and put a smile on my face. It felt like getting raped over and over again but I had to allow it.

I started by sitting with my clients before each visit getting to know them, it was my way of not feeling like a prostitute I felt at least I knew them a little bit.

When I first started to get to know my clients a lot had the same story the same lies. See the enemy is not brilliant he uses the same lies the same schemes on all of us. They said they loved their wives and their family but were starving emotionally, mentally and physically.

Listening to the same stories their wife hasn't touched them in years, they still have needs some of their wives telling them to go get it somewhere else just don't bring it home.

And yes, I saw men who were addicted to sex …Christians and non-Christians lost in their own desires. Addiction is the killer sent from the enemy to kill, steal and destroy.

I could see how empty they were I could feel their pain even in all the sin. As husbands and wives, we need to keep the bedroom light burning just because you may have lost your desire does not mean your partner has.

I had to learn what real intimacy was in God's eyes, what a sexual relationship meant as a Christian. God created all these pleasure zones in and on our body for exactly that "pleasure". Now going so far to the dark side of sexuality and lust, I needed to find out what was God's will. After praying about it I asked God to show me how I was supposed to be with my future husband because being an escort affected my view of intimacy and I needed truth. I love a good romance movie from time to time, I think because I still believe love like that can exist lol but one that is in union with God.

The partners I choose lacked any idea how to be intimate. They thought they were manly men, the kind that think that if I am still with you, that means I love you. I was always left scurrying around like a mouse looking for any crumbs I could get. Words of affirmation are my strongest in my love language, so not getting any was a slow painful death in these relationships.

So now I am studying Songs of Solomon WOW!!!

Now not to be rude or out of line but this is by far the best porn I have come across. The intimacy and passion, unity is what I want in my marriage.

Consummation of Love

The opening lines of Song of Songs 5 express the consummation of the lover's relationship. The lover is here expressing the exhilaration and joy of their union, but the pleasure is not his alone. The Beloved also expresses her pleasure (SS 6:2-3) The love they share is not just emotional or physical. The Lover calls his Beloved "my sister, my bride "(SS 5:1), and the Beloved also expresses her pleasure (SS 5:16) These two are experiencing what is meant to be one of the significant blessings of marriage, deep, intimate friendship with each other. When the foundation of a marriage is an abiding friendship, which includes mutual respect and care, a marriage can weather most any storm.

Again, and again the Lover and his Beloved praise each other. She is truly captivated by his appearance and goes to great lengths to explain the delight she finds in every aspect of his physical beauty (SS 5:10-16). What are we to make of such an extravagant praise? First, the enjoyment of the physical body of one's spouse is a gift from God. Within the secure covenant of marriage, the bodies of a husband and wife can be seen, touched, enjoyed and admired. Second, with this couple, praise and enjoyment flow both ways. Each one is free to enjoy and be enjoyed. Third, beyond the enjoyment of another's body is the steadfast heart connection they share. They are united to each other, as ever loyal ever-loving friends.

As husbands and wives, we need to protect our partners from our words and our thoughts. They are not the enemy it's easy to spew all the negative things we are dealing with, and what we say we call into existence in and outside the bedroom.

You need to guard your heart and their heart too! It is so easy to want justice when we are feeling vulnerable and feel hurt. We need to set our troubles and worry at the altar. Allow God to do his glory in our relationships we are his children nothing changes circumstances as much as God can.

It all starts with a willing open heart and total faith in God that he knows best for us a total submission. God loves us so much he does not want us the same. He wants to break the rebellion in us, growing in faith, love and forgiveness always. None of us has arrived it's a daily journey of giving our will over to God dying to our flesh.

Chapter Four

Rahab New Future For A Woman
With A Seedy Past

Here is the story of a woman who was a prostitute in the Bible who was living a life, not in his will, it's never too late to come back to the throne no matter how far off we have been led and lured away from God.

Here is a story of unshakable faith from an incredible woman of God.

Rehab a new future for a woman with a past

It wasn't unusual for strange men to appear at her door. She was, after all, a prostitute.

The Israelite spies came to Rehab looking for a place to hide, and they put their lives in her hands.

Who could have failed to hear about the Israelites? They had been in the desert for 40 years and now we're heading straight towards Jericho.

But Rahab told the spies she had heard of the God of Israel and the deeds he had done on behalf of his people.

It was as if she was just waiting for evidence of Him in her own life. When she saw the chance, she did not hesitate. She joined the cause of this God whom she believed to be greater than the Gods worshipped by her people "for the Lord your God in heaven and on the earth below" Jos 2:11

What if these men betrayed her? What if their God failed her? There could be no turning back. Risking her own death, she was obedient to the conviction of truth within her - no debate, no consultation, no wavering.

Within minutes of her decision, Rahab revealed her extraordinary heart.

Rahab interceded for her family's safety as well as her own. Her family heeded her, for when the walls of Jericho came down, her relatives were with her!

Over the ensuing years, Rahab surely needed to learn a new way of relating to men. Perhaps her restoration required the greatest faith of all, everyday choices, without drama or spotlight, to be chaste, to forgive, to trust again.

Scripture reveals that she continued to hold on to God who gave her a new beginning.

Mathew 1:5 lists Rahab among the forebears of Jesus. But she is not called "the prostitute" for the stigma of her past is overshadowed by the honour given her by God. And by choosing her a gentle sinner God confirms that he is the Saviour of all peoples, for all time and all circumstances.

Is there hope for a woman with a past, someone who has made bad decisions and given herself to a life of sin? Yes, he has given me that hope restores in my soul ...to every rotten root that has manifested itself in my life, he restores it with new life, new roots, his roots.

Our enemy wants us to believe that nothing good can come from such a wreckage. But Rahab's life demonstrates the benefits of believing God instead. When Rahab choose Him, he gave her a completely new life. And he set no limits on her potential as his child. None.

I had to learn about my new blueprint God designed for my life. What were my inner deep desires that he made in me? When you get a new computer, you learn all the components it has. All the things it is capable of doing and has a guide and instructions on how to use it.

God has given us that in His Word and in The Holy Spirit. Ask Holy Spirit to reveal to you how you are made in His likeness, ask Him how to obtain all the things you need to glorify Him.

One of the best things I ever did was learn my own love language. The five love languages by (Gary Chapman)

It helped me to learn about what I needed and how to obtain it.

Remembering before being in a marriage where I was starved on every level after getting divorced. I kept making the same mistakes with the men I choose I did not see my own worth and I was a four out of ten when I rated myself.

I now sit at a solid 8 with God showing me through his merciful eyes all I had in me. I was meant to shine bright, not choose partners where my light intimidated them but loved that about me!

Don't let your shine dim for anyone even if your energy is too much for someone you're wasting your full potential. You were meant to shine, own it, God will put you where you are needed and appreciated.

My last relationship I was forced to dim my shine. I could not get very excited when Jesus was showing himself to me, the absolute best high ever! But I was sharing it with the wrong person and he would say to me why are you so wired? Sit down chill out relax. I realized I was trying to shrink myself to fit into this little box he wanted me in. I was dying on every level snuffing out my flame.

When that happened, it left me feeling ashamed and took the wind out of my sails very quickly

Mathew 7:6

Do not give dogs what is sacred, do not throw your pearls to pigs. If you do, they may trample them under their feet, and then turn and tear you to pieces.

Being in that toxic relationship for two years caused me to hit my ultimate rock bottom. I stayed because of all my insecurities I did not know my worth. I had met him being an escort he wanted things sexually that I knew were not of God but because I was living the life of a prostitute I had learned to quiet the voice of Holy Spirit. I am a people pleaser, I was choosing to please him instead of God

Because of God's Mercy and Grace for me for all of us, he started bringing his light into the situation. I no longer wanted to provide these things to this man. The thought of being with him sexually started to repulse me. To the point I could no longer give myself to him any longer I was done. God made it done when I did not have my own strength, God made me courageous giving me a backbone I didn't even realize. What I had thought was a man I would marry one day spend the rest of my days with God hardened my heart towards him because I did not have the strength to do it. God wasn't done yet, by meditating on the great victorious woman in the Bible. The woman God created me to be. he started instilling in me an integrity for myself when men would once make crude jokes I would be the first to join in, now I despised it.

God started to replace all the wrong thinking and feelings I had in my life. With his right-thinking his feelings, his love for me and all the others out there stuck. Pray Holy Spirit replaces all the wrong with his truth, his truth sets us free!

Ephesians 5:22-24

To submit to accept or yield to a superior force or will of another person there have been times in many lives where I could not care for myself wracked with depression and anxiety, addiction, shame and a battlefield in my mind, heart and soul.

When I was choosing to live in the world and I choose to not deal with the pain that needed addressing, and when I felt it coming I ran to food, drugs, alcohol, sex to numb out. Not trusting my Lord and Savior paid the cost of all those sins but my own flesh and the rebellious spirit was struggling to give it all to

I needed to completely let go cut all those strongholds out and replace them with the truth.

I needed to yield to my superior force my Lord and Savior. God show me your ways and let my flesh drown.

He called me to be still and know that he is God. While writing this book showing me I needed to be still with Him the more obedient I became with Him the more revelations I received. The more time I spent with Him, the more the new came out soothing off my old skin, my old beliefs, my old habits.

Saying is true you become the person you spend the most time with and I was seeing God's heart his goodness. It came to the point I didn't want to be in the darkness anymore when I choose to stay in his presence I was filled with his light. And like a toddler takes it first steps that toddler depends on its parent. In time as soon as I even headed into the darkness I couldn't go, I was finally at peace, I was in total freedom in Him.

After listening to a Joel Osteen sermon on "God uses the seasons of silence to get us prepared." I realized I have been in a season of silence with God. I have for the past four months, what I thought was punishment is not. He is changing me on the inside on so many levels. The more time I spend with Him, he shows me the areas I need to change for Him to use me for everything he has planned. My flesh needs to be crucified.

I have been wanting to get baptized. I have the yearning to have all the men I have had to be intimate with, all my addictions I want them washed clean from my past. When I called my church and inquired about it they said they didn't have any planned yet but will get back to me when they do. I was disappointed my first response was to pout, but Lord! I need this! But getting in my silent place with God where I am a work in progress, he gently says not yet, trust me. And I do.

Yesterday was a day filled with God in praise and prayer. Today I woke up in a bad miserable mood in my spirit feeling sorry for myself. Thinking I am stuck in this apartment night and day, I have given up my friends that choose to stay in their fleshly lifestyles. My whole life as I knew it, I stay here trying to be obedient as I can Lord! I am lonely and bored my old flesh would say screw it I am going out and getting drunk, I could feel that spirit come on me, but I did not know what I was feeling except impatience and anger.

I did the only thing I knew I put praise and worship on and started to lift my hands to Him. I had my phone in one and my vape for quitting smoking in the other. I started singing to Him again, then he said now the vape put it down. I was like really Lord? He then gently showed me the things I needed to change and showed me my rebellious spirit. As soon as the revelation was brought forth it hit my heart that this is exact truth.

It was like I received a gift God showed me what my battle was, and in these past few months, he has been getting my heart right and now I find the tools I need in his word to break these strongholds.

I can't have it MY way all the time. I have to trust Him with my "whole" life and on his understanding and timing. I have never desired the need to become this obedient ever to this level. But he is renewing my soul each day I am getting stronger and healing I am becoming the woman God intended.

I am in a moulting phase right now God is peeling all the layers off me, one layer at a time. This book has been so healing for me.

There are days when I can feel the rebellion rise, I cling to God as the attacks on my mind come hard at me.

What's your responsibility in your rock bottom? How did you hinder your growth? Staying in a relationship you know Jesus did not want you in? Staying in an addiction, not having total faith in Him? Pride, rebellion? Ask Jesus to show you where you are in bondage.

Exodus 20 2-6

I am the Lord your God, who brought you out of Egypt, out of the land of slavery. (Ask God to show you where you are still in slavery? Pride, gambling, sex?)

You shall have no other Gods before me. (What are you putting before God?)

49

You shall not make for yourself an idol in the form of anything in heaven above or in the waters below. You shall not bow down to them or worship them, for I the Lord your God am a jealous God, punishing the children for the sin of the fathers to the third and fourth generation of those who hate me., but showing love to a thousand generations of those who keep my commandments.

(I know my idols pride, jealousy, sex, drugs, alcohol, men, food and more the Lord is showing me. I need to die to my flesh no holding back anymore give up all my vices. It is Saturday night never being single would I be home alone in my ponytail and sweats content with my date with Jesus tonight but here I am)

Having to struggle through the temptation of wanting to tap out is so overwhelming it brings me to tears. But I must keep fighting I can feel attacks from the enemy he does not want to have this book out there helping souls for Jesus. I can't let the fear win, I am so emotionally spent I have isolated myself with God I felt in my heart I needed house arrest with the Holy Spirit. I am raw, vulnerable and lonely, but I will persevere. When the yearning for my old ways flood me, battle me I am making it a habit to just stay still and know he is my God. To not give in to the old vices that I thought brought me peace. I so used to live in my flesh being a yes woman to everyone and everything.

1 Corinthians 13: 4

Love is patient, love is kind. It does not envy, it does not boast, it is not proud. It is not self-seeking, it is not easily angered, it keeps no record of wrongs.

Love does not delight in evil but rejoices with the truth. It always perseveres.

James 5:7

Be patient then brothers, until the Lord's coming. See how the farmer waits for the land to yield its valuable crop and how patient he is for the autumn and spring rains. You too be patient and stand firm, because the Lord's coming is near. Don't grumble against each other brothers or you will be judged. The Judge is standing at the door.

Brothers, as an example of patience in the face of suffering, take the prophets who spoke in the name of the Lord. As you know, we consider blessed those who have persevered. You have heard Job's perseverance and have seen what the Lord finally brought about.

The Lord is full of compassion and mercy for all of us.

I have fallen short so many times in my life. Where shame and condemnation from the enemy nailed me, but then Jesus softly leads me back to Him.

And I ask Holy Spirit to show me how to have a submissive heart, a servant heart, his heart. To submit my will to Him to submit to his way, not to submit to the world for all the wrong things. Because of the rebellion in me God had to show me what it meant to submit his way to allow myself to be vulnerable not in fear but total freedom. I pray for God to get my heart right to receive what he calls me to do.

Ephesians 5 25-33

We are called to submit ourselves to one another for the sake of Christ husbands, wives, children, singles.... Christ has the paid the ultimate sacrifice to save us, therefore, we will submit to our brothers and sisters in the Lord out of that love. We love and submit because Christ first loved us. A husband loving the interaction with his wife will produce a willing submission to him a husband who cares for his wife's total growth his commitment to make her holy by cleansing her in the word and to present her to himself as a radiant church shining bright, illuminated, glowing, incandescent.

Without blemish but holy and blameless in this same way husbands ought to love their wives as their own bodies. He who loves himself loves his wife for this reason a man shall leave his mother and father and be united to his wife and the two shall become of one flesh, vessel.

I was married for sixteen years I was stuck in a marriage of religion, oppression, and no growth in any area.

I had left my marriage twice the first time was coming clean after getting addicted to crack cocaine. I was totally addicted to three months. I had my own hair salon in my basement, I still maintained my life I worked and took care of my family.

Once everyone was sleeping I would leave to go get my fix after three months I knew I needed help

I went home and the next day I told my ex-husband I needed to go in for help. I will never forget the look of disgust and disappointment on his face. I asked for him to take me to the hospital so I could go to rehab. He had no idea what I was doing what I had been up to when we are addicts we become the best liars and manipulators.

He took me and when I got their God's grace again they sent me to a detox. I remember pulling up to the front in the worse area in the city. Fear overwhelmed me I asked my husband to bring me inside, he looked at me and said you got yourself in this you get yourself out.

I cried my eyes out but I knew I needed to do this, I found a strength in me to walk out of that truck and not look back.

I spent 10 days in that place then 3 months in rehab! One of the best things I did for myself and for my children.

But after six months of being on my own with my kids and the pressure from others that I was being selfish. I caved in and went back to my ex who never asked me the first time or the last to stay, he was full of pride we had seen five marriage counsellors. But I went back and as soon as I got the kids on the bus and him off to work I fell apart I knew I settled again I stayed for another seven years till I left for good.

Lots of times I almost caved and went back because I felt bad for him, but a friend reminded me if I went back nothing would change. I gave it my all it came down it was either him or me, I choose me.

Early on in my Christianity, I learned from a mentor that as woman we set the thermostat in our lives and in our home!

Society has put a number on when a woman should get married have children ding ding ding the clock is ticking.

Choosing the right partner is so important marriage is one of the most beautiful exchanges between two people.

But when you get it wrong it can be a prison. Know your worth find a Godly partner that will build you up and protect your heart and soul! And YES, they still exist out there perhaps you have been surrounding yourselves with all the wrong ones!

I have a list of the qualities I need in my future husband which I worked through with my counsellor. My future husband will be a man of God who knows who he is in Christ.

Here is my list ask Holy Spirit to help you write out your future husband's qualities. This way if an imposter comes in again you have it written down as facts. You can go to that list and ask yourself with God's will, does this man have the things I seek?

- Man after God's heart
- Integrity, loyal, humble, patient.
- Empathetic, caring, thoughtful, humble
- Compassionate, courteous, excellent hygiene, outgoing
- Adventurous, financially secure, great sense of humour
- Takes pride in his appearance
- Seeks a healthy lifestyle
- Thankful, grateful, appreciative
- Gets my love language
- Sexually virility takes initiative, passionate, playful.
- Similar interests, open minded, positive, a visionary, secure, confident, accepting.

I had to know what I deserved what God wanted me to have. What my future husbands "computer" would contain in it!

Even though I was living in sin... God still kept me. I still prayed, I know some of you will say you were a prostitute God would have no part of you. Sorry but that is just another lie. Yes, I was living in sin, I was an adulterer, I was a "woman at the well".

But it is written ....

Psalm 145:18

The Lord is near to all who call on Him, to all who call on Him in truth.

Becoming an escort carried shame upon me I was just living to survive to help my kids and always in the back of my mind how to get out. And I called on the Lord.

I became very isolated and stuck by myself. I met Glen very early on he was one of my first clients. God still brought people into my life to help me, right from the beginning till the end he brought them and finally delivered me from that life.

When I met Glenn, I was so new to everything. I was using my own phone and my real name. He explained I need a work phone and a stage name. I was so naive about it all I would tell them my real name real phone number with my name displaying even then God was protecting me.

I continued to work from a hotel for a couple months and I met Don. After chatting with him he told me he knew this girl that has an apartment downtown she works from when she comes in from another city and was looking to share the apartment.

The next day we met at the apartment it was beautiful and discreet. I got settled in and began to build up my clientele base. But months later when I did meet her I found out, unfortunately, she was an alcoholic and heavy drug user.

I recently found out that she died from her addiction. I still remember the first time I saw her shoot up and then she asked if I wanted a hit. I tried sharing Jesus with her but when she would rage she would spew the ugliest things about me and Him. Even then I allowed Jesus to use me to share the Gospel I never turned away from Him in all my rebellion. But I never fully gave it all up for Him either, living one foot in the world and one foot in the grave.

Got to the point I could not be around her I felt guilty but God gently pushed me forward. I had to leave her behind I shared the Gospel she chooses to not be saved. We are not called to save everyone we all have a free will and yes, it's our responsibility to share the Gospel, but when you've done all you can. Walk on and continue to pray for them, there is someone out there waiting and ready to hear leave it to God.

Mathew 7:6

Do not give dogs what is sacred, do not throw your pearls before pigs. If you do, they will trample them under their feet, and turn and tear you to pieces.

She had been in the industry that is what we call it and I was an SP "service provider".

But life had not been kind to her she was bitter and broken.

I would listen to how we were supposed to be with clients. Get them in and out as quickly as possible treat them like tricks or Johns, I knew that wasn't right.

After a year of dealing with her, it was a constant battle. I had no income to claim but I was the one paying for the apartment because all her money went to drugs.

So, I talked to my landlord and she let me rent my own apt there so I got away from the madness.

Don moved on and so did I. Holy Spirit is pushing me to bring this point home. Even though I choose to be in this sin God did not forsake me. If I had stayed in that hotel room working, I know it would have consumed me. When I was working from a hotel I felt even dirtier I had no discretion. I would take clients all night, that meant the worse ones. The ones at the bar, all the gang bangers. Once I got settled in my apartment, I needed to be discreet so I only seen limited respectful clients from 9 am till 8 pm. I didn't want to bring attention to myself, doing that brought me a much safer clientele.

There was this young man that came to see me once I could tell how nervous he was. After sitting with him he told me he was married with four small kids I asked why he came to me? He told me his friends put him up to it.

I asked him if his wife was still sexual with him he replied yes.

I asked him why he would risk it after talking to him for a while I convinced him to go home to his family and to not do this again. A few hours later he sent me a text with a pic of him and his family saying thank you!

I have had men ask me to remove my cross I wear around my neck. I refuse to I am never ashamed to share the love of Jesus.

I have been asked how I can justify what I did and remain a Christian. I don't have the answers I just know Jesus has redeemed me and he continues too.

I try to have a humble heart and to love people through the eyes of Jesus!

No judgment just acceptance for I know how hard the struggle is at times, in those times I need Jesus, love and encouragement. We all do.

I know many people will judge my actions. I leave my life and salvation at the cross with Jesus. My God is forgiving, loving and merciful. We will all fall short, some of us more than others. For that reason, Peter is the one I most connect with out of all Jesus's disciples. Peter's failures give me hope. That when I wander off my path God is waiting for me to come and say Father forgive me I'm lost again please put me back on my path with you.

Lamentations 3:22-23

Because of the Lord's great love, we are not consumed, for his compassions never fail. They are new every morning, great is your faithfulness.

If I allowed myself to listen and believe the lies of the enemy I would not be where I am today!

My shame and regret would swallow me up. When God put on my heart to write this book I said Lord I am not worthy, and they will judge me. His reply was showing me as I am in his eyes forgiven, redeemed, cleansed of my sins.

Chapter Five

Faithful Cleansed Daughter

One day when I was riding in a cab. Jesus gave me a vision of myself. He cleansed me put oil on my feet and forehead dressed me in the finest linen. Jewels and a crown of glory! He presented me to everyone as his faithful, cleansed daughter! He showed me through his eyes who I was.

Then close to finishing my book he gave me another one where we are being blinded by our own sexual immorality.

When false teachings get a foothold in our lives and sexual immorality sets In, it's the sin that starts to separate us from God.

Pornography, sexually explicit videos, photographs, writings, or the like, whose purpose is to elicit sexual arousal.

Being in the Sex Industry it was my goal to elicit men. On top of being an escort, I was also a Dominatrix and Fetish Specialist. When I searched the word elicit this is what I found. "Educe, evoke, extract, extort "mean" to draw something hidden, latent, or reserved. Educe implies the bringing out of something potential or latent meaning (of a quality or state) existing but not yet developed or manifested, hidden, concealed.

The day before God brought to light the darkness I still had in me that was diming his light, robbing my peace. I had been praying in the Spirit for months now throughout the day when I didn't know what to pray or no energy to pray. I prayed in the Spirit (tongues).

My spirit was restless so I did what calmed me now instead of drugs or men or booze I ran a bubble bath. I could feel the rebellious spirit in me rise. I started praying to Holy Spirit to show me where these men fell short being enslaved to all their lusts. I began to pray in the Spirit I had never experienced anything like what was about to happen. I started to pray and my words came with urgency like I have never witnessed. I couldn't take breaths deep enough or fast enough to get it all out. I felt such a deep heartache so deep in me an uncontrollable sadness. I felt like it was being ripped from me I couldn't get any more out deep dry heaving sobs, then a peace washed over me. I asked Holy Spirit to give me eyes that are open to see. Ears that can hear and can distinguish his truth and the lies of the enemy. I felt he was at work with me preparing my heart to receive it.

On that same afternoon, I had an appointment within walking distance. I had got into the habit of listening to worship music when I walked on my phone. I looked everywhere for twenty minutes and could not find it. It finally came down to the second I had to go! Then again Holy Spirit trust me to come alone without it. In my mind I am like are you kidding me no phone for two hours it's not possible Lord! Trust me he urged me. Fine Lord Let's go…. I felt like a baby off the bottle so I started praying. Lord show me what I need to see let me know it as truth. As I am walking I start to hear this distinct voice talking and laughing like I was listening in on a conversation then the Holy Spirit asked me do you hear his voice? Yes, I reply it sounded familiar but not for anyone I knew. You worry constantly about the fear of not knowing when you will meet your future husband that voice you hear, that is him you will know without a single doubt who he is. As soon as he speaks you will both know!

Goosebumps even while writing this. And its true fear is gone I know now how I will know! Thank you, Jesus! If I would have had my phone I would have been distracted by my music or Facebook. I would have missed out on this revelation. I've come to depend on Him for every single thing in my life. His way is so much better, his love for me overflows my heart to the point it surpasses all my old understanding and misbeliefs.

God still at work in me I began to pray in the Spirit and prayed when that deep pitted sobbing came fast and sudden a sadness and deep-rooted mourning like a death. I felt to the absolute core of my being. I kept praying show me where all this is coming from. Now I heard of prophesying never experienced but throughout this journey, I had one prayer partner. My Peter I will explain about this amazing man of God in a bit but this truth needs to be brought out of the darkness on the subject of sexual slavery and the world of BDSM (Bondage, Domination, and Sadomasochism) Sadism "a sexual perversion in which gratification is obtained by the infliction of physical or mental pain on others, delight in cruelty."

Before becoming an Escort and Dominatrix the BDSM world had always frightened me. I was very naïve to it all. I just knew that the darkness it contained and what I would allow myself to be drawn into would change my look and feel of true intimacy forever. Being an escort was enslaving being able to disconnect from God to do my "job" more easily but with it was bringing death to my spiritual intimacy with God. I started researching the effects it was having on the people that were becoming addicted to it. I came upon the interview that Dr. James Dobson had with serial killer hours before his execution. He went on to explain how his growing addiction to porn brought him to do the unspeakable things he did. He claims he was a normal person and gradually once he becomes addicted to it, he wanted more and more extreme hardcore visuals he wants to make a reality. Now my understanding of it is very true of that. My clientele that I was marketing after all were the perverse the thrill seekers of wanting more excitement in their sexual lives. To bring them into my world of fantasy and promising that I could make their deepest and darkest fantasies a reality. And I did, now when I was researching the things these men were craving. I watched and learned from BDSM porn, although I did not have likeminded interests in this fantasy world. I became their tour guide into the darkness, and each time I did I told myself it was harmless play, I was so deceived by now. After being in it for a while I never allowed myself to ask why these men wanted these disgusting and volatile things done to them? Who was I to judge was my answer. I would ask them a few questions before I started a session how you started out getting interested in BDSM. All of them answered the same question Porn and that things in the bedroom were stale they craved the need to explore. I would then take them through an obstacle course of their deepest desires.

I have received deliverance in these unspeakable things I have done. Once the truth was brought before me and my eyes were opened to all God's truth on it. I repented forgive me, Father. I was still living in my apartment that I had worked from I had two bedrooms. I had just closed the door to my "work" room, I felt the heaviness of sin in it. Holy Spirit started to speak to me. He kept putting that room on my mind. I finally recognized the feeling of fear. I prayed Lord take it all, break in me all that has to go to live in your perfect will in my life.

He instructed me to get ready like I use too for a client. But Lord I replied I'm tired and don't have the energy to do it. It's pointless, my rebellious spirit leering its ugly head. He is a persistent God, Thank God! He instructed me to get ready as if getting ready for my best review I was going to get from a client. My ugly rebellion fighting still, and my uneasiness of not wanting to go back to that dark place. I needed some type of confirmation I texted my prayer partner Peter explaining to him what The Holy Spirit was asking me to do. He went into straight-up encouragement. Praying strength and courage for me telling me God will not leave me. So, began my redemption. I had a shower the longest shower I have ever had in my life. I washed my hair three times scrubbed my body, shaved two times finally when I felt I was clean enough I got out and proceeded to get ready.

Holy Spirit was urging me to have wine. I was refraining from alcohol so I text Peter and told him. His reply "communion wine, the last supper." I obeyed I poured a glass of wine and went to my prayer spot. I began to pray, he urged me to get a cracker I obeyed and came back to my prayer spot. I then had communion with The Lord, he gave me instructions that I was to get my workroom ready light candles. I kept seeing the number five- three times in three different areas. I text Peter and asked him if the number five meant anything to him? Because it did not to me, he texts back Yes! That is my lucky number I received a bible in Sunday school for five years of perfect attendance. Confirmation for me to proceed God knew I needed a witness

I went and lit the candles I felt a familiar presence and it was not God's I knew who it was. That room was bringing such a fear in me that I was unable to go into it. But I needed my shoes from that room. I took a deep breath and went in. I was drawn to the candles so I went to them I had them lit on three different shelves in the same row. I began to count them the first shelf had six the second six and the third six, 666 the mark of the beast. I ran out of there my hair on the back of my neck was standing, I was scared to the very core of me.

I text Peter and told him he's here the beast was here. He texts back God is right beside you! You are strong Amelia! I needed the shoes in the closet in that room. The closet was what scared me the most about that room because I used it as a glory hole. But I was terrified like a child, I finally came to realize I had to complete what God had ordained in front of me. I went into the room and as soon as I got to the closet the loudest thump hit the window. I ran out of there in pure terror! I texted Peter I can't do this! He texts Pray and God's angels are protecting you.

I put the full armour of God on and went into that room. I closed the door behind me, I walked over to a bench and sat and waited. I felt an anger rise in me that I have never experienced in my life I stood up and screamed at the enemy you perverted Liar. I am taking back everything you have stolen from me! My innocence, my integrity, my worth. I no longer am your slave!

I am coming for every lie you have ever made me believe! And my God in heaven is going to make good on every broken promise I believed from you! I am coming for the slaves that are still shackled in your perverted filth.

Their eyes are going to be opened to your perversion. I know how you're deceiving them and I am binding you to the word of God! All these empty tormenting vessels are going to flow with the Blood of Jesus Christ! In his name, I pray over this room that nothing that is not of Him, I demand in the authority given to me in Christ you go back to hell where you belong!

Satan blinds us in sexual perversion by bringing false teachers that make light of it. The lying sneaky enemy thinks he's sly, look at magazines in grocery stores. Look on every cover all relating on how to have the best sex of your life, the clothing they wear does not leave much to the imagination.

Jude 1:12

These men are blemishes at your love feasts, eating with you without the slightest qualm, Sheppard's who only feed themselves. They are clouds without rain, blown along by the wind, autumn trees, without fruit and uprooted, twice dead. They are wild waves of the sea, foaming up their shame, wandering stars, for whom blackest darkness has been reserved forever.

1 Corinthians 6:18

Flee from sexual immorality, all other sins a man commits are outside his body, but he who sins sexually sins against his own body. Do you not know that your body is a temple of the Holy Spirit, who is in you, whom you have received from God? You are not your own, you were bought for a price. Therefore, honour God with your body.

I fell to the ground I felt all the sin that sexual immorality brought. I asked for forgiveness for my rebellious spirit be snuffed out. I waited I got clear instruction to undress out of the harlot clothing I had on. I obeyed I sat in the middle of the room and felt such peace and love rush over me. I felt like I had been cleansed from the inside out.

Then the Holy Spirit began to speak to me, you are cleansed and forgiven by the blood of Jesus. You will keep yourself in purity till I present you to your husband, and I am preparing his heart to receive you. That room is now my prayer room, my favourite room in my whole apartment I had the blinds closed, and a black curtain on the window, when I took off the curtain and opened the blinds, I discovered the most breathtaking view of my city, the river and all of downtown.

See how God is so good, that room was full of sin, regret, shame. He restored it to beyond what I could have imagined!

That day in that room has meant the death of my flesh, dying to my rebellious spirit, redemption. I am coming for the slaves still stuck in the bondage of sexual lusts and addictions. I pray that your eyes are open to see and ears to hear the truth. Amen

Up until now, I haven't shared about a "Peter" brought into my life from God. I never knew how to explain it until now. While I was offering Fetish and Kink sessions I met a man let's refer to him as" Peter" he was a client for two years. Around a year into our relationship, God started to put an urgency on me to ask about his faith we sat for a couple hours talking and sharing. He told me how he believed but wasn't really living for God. He explained how he had been quite spiritual at one point in his life.

But life just had a way of taking over with all the responsibility he had been given caring for his family. His daughter was going through a nasty separation from her husband. His daughter and his granddaughter had moved home with him and his wife. God showed me the role he was meant to play in his granddaughter's life. My grandfather who was very present in my life had passed away when I was ten in an accident at work. I still remember the role he played in my life. He was a non-believer and an alcoholic but his love for me was endless.

He instilled in me his love for me, he told me I was a swan his patience was unending with me. I loved being in his presence and even though he was a violent, drunk, he never was once with me. The amazing thing is that he was not my biological grandfather. He was my granny's second husband but he took me and loved me as if I was his own.

We were made for such boldness in Him, my prayer for you is that you have a heart that yearns to know Him, to give your life to Him. All of it the good, the bad and yes even more so the shameful stuff you need deliverance in. He's waiting to show you all he can do when you seek Him.

What happens to the ones who never seek or obtain it? They lose out on a life in Him that is so glorified, His peace and His love flow through you like fountains of refreshing water healing your soul. I want that so badly for you all!

Peter began to visit me twice a week, we would get into in-depth conversations about Jesus. God began to show us how real he was and is in our lives. God knew I needed just one Peter to get me through this book, to get me out of prostitution. The more we prayed for each other and our families the more our faith raised. We both changed into what he had planned his will be done in our lives we prayed. We would encourage each other with verses and online sermons about God! I was able to share with Peter how I never wanted to do this when I was a little girl swinging on the swings I never imagined this.

Finally, being delivered from escorting I was praying I had a client that was coming soon during all my sessions before I had found a switch that I could turn off when I had to do my Job. But I couldn't find it. I was left in that room, not my persona I couldn't find her! I text Peter explaining my situation. That I was unable to do it any longer, he replied "Praise Jesus! That was when the intimacy of our flesh was crucified with each other. That's when we became brother and sister in Christ. I was panicked how am I going to survive? My kids!

He reassured me everything was going to be okay, I had to have faith! When I hurt my knee and was down he mentioned how I had time now and maybe I should consider taking this time and write a book about my redemption. I was floored I explained to him and showed him my laptop and the two years previous I opened up a file showing him I had started a book it only had a title 'The Naughty Secrets of An Escort". God showed Peter that seed I had in me about writing a book, but a book to glorify his name and all his goodness now instead!

I was breaking and broken, God kept pressing Peter to help me get by, to finish this book. He put an amount of money on Peter's heart when he came to visit he handed me an envelope in it contained the exact amount of money I would need to survive on till I completed this book no more and no less! I was free from having to worry about money and focus on this book and heal from all the trauma I put myself through. The faith this man has is inconceivable, he has been my encourager, my prayer warrior, my friend. And one of the most obedient men with integrity I've ever witnessed with my own eyes.

His sharing with me the miracle of helping set me free. How has all this impacted his life? God took an indiscretion on his part and turned it into a situation that glorified Him! He knows in the deepest part of his heart we were never meant to be lovers. We have a divine connection is what he calls it, and I agree! Had he never met me God's Holy Spirit may not have come alive in him. I may have ended up on the streets addicted to drugs which I know would have been the death of me. When you think every avenue for that miracle you are waiting for is closed. Be still and know he is God. Being still means don't act on impulse or feelings. When you don't know what to do just be still in his presence He will renew you, direct you.

Chapter Six

A Wife of Noble Character

God had so much to damage to work through with me. I'm sure if I could see myself, I must have looked like a two-year-old having tantrums. I had to allow Him and trust Him, I had no clue on the woman I was supposed to be. I had been a harlot for five years. I prayed God show me…God had to show me what it meant to be a Wife noble of character he needs to prepare my heart get rid of the damage that has been done being rebellious to Him. Seeking his truth on the type of woman he created me to be.

Proverbs 31:10-13

> A wife of noble character who can find?
> She is worth far more than rubies.
> Her husband has full confidence in her and lacks
>   nothing of value.
> She brings him good, not harm, all the days of
>   her life.

She selects wool and flax and works with eager hands.

(Think about this she is out in the marketplace as the CEO of her household. She is wise and business minded and confident. Her husband trusts her as the vice president of their household. His nurturing and the high esteem he holds her too, allows her to blossom daily. Gaining more wisdom and knowledge being the best she can be and to be a blessing to those all around her.)

Proverbs 31:14-20

She is like the merchant ships, bringing her food from afar.

She gets up while it is still dark, she provides for her family, and portions for her servant girls.

She considers a field and buys it; out of her earnings, she plants a vineyard.

She sets about her work vigorously; her arms are strong for her tasks.

She sees that her trading is profitable, and her lamp does not go out at night.

In her hand, she holds the distaff and grasps the spindle with her fingers.

> She opens her arms to the poor and extends
> her hands to the needy. (What a glorious
> site to love purely no judgment to the less
> fortunate she has a servant heart, no ego just
> God-confidence and love!)

Proverbs 31 21-22

When it snows she has no fear for her household, for all of them are clothed in scarlet.

She makes coverings for her bed, she is clothed in fine linen and purple.

(Sorry for the interruption but this has to come out into the light and I am one who fell into its ugly trap. Ladies when our lovely husbands marry us we were still presenting well lol. As in we still, put energy into presenting ourselves the best way we could. Then comes kids and work and exhaustion but ladies don't let yourself go you are settling, for less than you can be. Bring out the lingerie again!)

Proverbs 31 23-

Her husband is respected at the city gate, where he takes his seat among the elders of the land. (she only speaks good of him she holds herself and him to the highest respect possible freely given not having to earn it.)

She makes linen garments and sells them. And supplies the merchants with sashes.

She is clothed with strength and dignity, she can laugh at the days to come.

She speaks with wisdom, and faithful instruction is on her tongue.

She watches over the affairs of her household and does not eat the bread of idleness.

Her children arise and call her blessed, her husband as well and he praises her.

Many women do noble things, but you surpass them all.

Charm is deceptive and beauty is fleeting, but a woman who fears the Lord is to be praised.

Give her the reward she has earned, and let her works bring her praise at the city gate.

WOW!!!!

If we read this detailed description of the ideal wife and mother as the point by point standard God expects us to live to, we are bound to feel overwhelmed and exhausted before we even begin!

The purpose of this epilogue to the book of Proverbs wasn't to give woman an unreachable to-do-list, but to spread out before them the many opportunities they have to use their gifts, talents and wisdom in fulfilling and productive ways.

Rather than limiting woman's roles, they are expanded endlessly. As woman, we are created to have a positive and profound impact on everyone around us, whether it be our husbands, children, parents, friends, clients, customers or society in general.

Being a woman is a blessing, and being a wise, strong and dignified woman blesses others in ways that can't be calculated.

A wife of noble character wears many faces and fills many roles that can change with the seasons of her life.

In essence, she draws her strength from the Lord to lay down her life for those she loves.

Her award?

Her children adore her, her husband cherishes her company, trusts her judgement and brags about her to all his friends.

She will be remembered long after she is gone, not as a woman who was beautifully knit a scarf or successfully manages her household, but as a woman who sought the Lord first.

Now, of course, circumstances are different if you are in an abusive relationship, again bring it to Jesus ask who you should talk to about your situation and get out if that is what you need to do.

I have been in a couple abusive relationships in my past, I was at such a low point in my life I thought that was what I deserved.

I was wrong and in God's timing and being patient, God will bring into my life the man He has created for me!

He is teaching me patience which is an area I have always struggled with.

When we are disobedient in our walk we are only making the journey longer, and more painful. When we choose to not die daily to our flesh we are stuck in the cycle. Jesus came to set the captives free are you still being held in bondage of destructive choices?

There were times God would remove a man in my life because he knew that was not my destiny. But I would get weak from loneliness and crawl and beg my way back.

The first incident God showed me this was after my separation from my husband. I got into a relationship with a non-believer who had five kids no relationship with any of them. For three years he lived with me not contributing any money for rent or food. It finally got to the point I couldn't' take another day of it. Begging him to get a job I got so frustrated after a fight with him one day I went for a drive. I pulled over cried my eyes out and finally said God help me I don't know what to do, please do SOMETHING! I went home and went to bed I woke up in the early morning to find him not in bed with me. I went downstairs to find him I walked into the kitchen and found his phone on the counter. I knew immediately something was wrong. I ran outside to the garage all his stuff was gone. No note couldn't call him I paid for his phone which is why he left it behind. I found out weeks later he went to Calgary 1400 miles away from me. God answered my prayer and removed that man from my life, knowing how weak willed I was. He took that man and put him out of my reach. But still, I yearned for him. I could see God smack his forehead and say my daughter, why can't you trust I know what is best for you.? I closed that door I hardened that man's heart towards you because you were not strong enough to stay away it is DONE!

But Lord I need him! My precious daughter the man I have for you, the path I am leading you down is far more glorious than you can possibly imagine. Are you ready to believe and follow me? Galatians 4:7-9

So, you are no longer a slave, but a son and since you are a son, God has made you an heir.

Formerly, when you did not know God, you were slaves to those who by nature are not God's.

But now you know God - rather are known by God- how is it that you are turning back to those weak and miserable principles?

Do you wish to be enslaved by them all over again?

We need to protect our hearts what we allow to absorb into our hearts is what we will reap. Do you know your worth? The people you choose to spend your time with pour their energy and beliefs on you. If you are on unsteady ground spiritually, mentally, emotionally be extra cautious who you allow speaking into your life. Ask God daily to show you how to put the armour of God on, to give you wisdom and knowledge on, who to be a blessing too. And those who are not ready to give you the discernment and strength to walk away.

I have been very careful who I share about writing this book with. I know I am sensitive and raw so I am only choosing to share with people I know share my vision., I cannot be shamed or convinced of not writing it this is God's will on my life. I also know the attacks from the enemy come hard and furious he knows his slaves are going to be set free!!! They will come to have their eyes opened to all understanding, ears and a heart be wide open to the Gospel. Amen.

Yes, we are meant to preach the Gospel and be a help to the broken hearted. But God showed me, certain people, I still had in my life, they were still in the world and I had to break free of the temptation of my old life. I was facing rejection from these people on my faith. And when I spent time with them I could feel the pull of my old self. I had to make a stand ….

Romans 16;17

I urge you, brothers to watch out for those who cause divisions and put obstacles in your way that are contrary to the teachings you have learned. Keep away from them. For such people are not serving our Lord Christ, but their own appetites. By smooth talk and flattery, they deceive the minds of naive people. Everyone has heard of your obedience, so I am overjoyed over you, but I want you to be wise about what is good, and innocent about what is evil.

Psalm 46:10

Be still and know I am God.

I had so many issues to work through, and the biggest one God is working on me now is being alone. I have spent my entire life having to have constant companionship. Learning to be still and patient I am getting stronger every day. I have never been on my own, I went from parent's home to my ex-husband. Up until over a year ago, I had a house that my son and daughter lived with me, now they are on their own and I am too.

I am getting comfortable in my own being, I still struggle with loneliness and times when my grief is unbearable I give it to Jesus. And he restores my purpose the fact that I haven't gone back to my old life again is a miracle in itself. And he is showing me that sometimes we have to leave the people we think we love behind for the cause of Christ.

All I know at this point is God has great things in my future and I am meant to be still right now. I dislocated my knee right before this journey with God began with this book. If I would not have got injured I would be out there trying to mask my pain with alcohol and bad choices that would have made things extremely worse.

Chapter Seven

Be Still And know I Am God

That night when I dislocated my knee was the beginning of my journey.

I laid awake in that bed for nine hours in excruciating pain until a friend finally answered and she brought me to the hospital. As I write this the tears are running down my face that is when God said to me you are going to learn what it means to be still and know I am God. This journey I am on is going to be to change my life. Did God do this to me? No, but he allowed it because that was the only way he could take this opportunity to be still with me.

For once in my life, I know my purpose and it happened when I gave my total life all of the bad and good over to God.

He is dealing with me on so many levels, I sit in gratitude and awe he is showing me who I really am and showing me where I fall short binding my strongholds, rebellion, destructive choices and setting me free.

What's your responsibility in your own rock bottom? As in how you are holding yourself back in your own destiny.

Mine is men always has been, not being able to be alone being co-dependent on any man willing to keep me, yes that was where my mindset was.

I am in a moulting stage right now ...

"How does one become a butterfly? She asked pensively

"You must want to fly so much that you are willing to give up being a caterpillar "

Trina Paulus

(Are you willing to give up all that is not God's will for your life?)

It's what we all wanted when we were children- to be loved and accepted exactly as we were then, not when we got taller or thinner or prettier…. And we still want it …. But we are not going to get it from other people until we can get it from ourselves.

Louise Hay

1 John 4:4

You dear children, are from God and have overcome them because the one who is in you is greater than the one who is already in the world.

I had put all my happiness on these men in my past relationships. Poured myself into them became their wife cleaned, cooked, did all their laundry, made their lunches I am a pleaser at heart but was pleasing the world not God.

But brothers and sisters in Christ, don't pour yourself into something that is not meant to be. Once you know your worth the cycle ends, and the YOU God intended you to break through boldly, confidently.

My insecurities came from choosing the wrong men I put all my worth in their incapable hands there is only one judge and juror are you listening and seeking wholeheartedly what our father says about you? What his plans are for your life?

Or are you staying in situations that hinder that? People are going to disappoint you, again and again, you got to know your worth and pray God's will be done in your life not your own. God keeps his promises!

Only then can you set the bar higher and have healthy boundaries and with God and the destiny that awaits you. It is your responsibility to stay on course, only you can choose to wake up every morning and get in prayer give everything over to the one person who has your back always has, he always will.

Once you experience that unconditional love and see yourself through God's eyes you rise, then he can turn your ashes into beauty. Once you see your worth through the eyes of Jesus is the absolute life changer you no longer have to settle again.

One definition of settling "when one chooses to become romantically involved with someone who is not as impressive, but just as simple to be with, as the best because it's easier."

I met my ex-husband at a bar when I was seventeen, moved in with him a few months later he was a drunk and an obnoxious one at that. Throw in a side of acid flashbacks into the mix very intense I thought awwwww I can love him, fix him. But this is the man who showed me Jesus I was an angry, raging atheist I hated God!

I thought he abandoned me I was so wrong he is a gentleman he does not force Himself on anyone he wants you to come to Him and he waiting with arms wide open.

Now listen to all my next relationships the same pattern of destruction.

Stayed in that marriage for thirty-six years trying to get my needs met from a man incapable of meeting them.

A couple more relationships same pattern they were wounded hurting men.

Prideful men that caused me to give up my self-worth too.

I became what their treatment was towards me. The more they pushed me away the more I begged the more self-control I lost the worse it would get. I was always left feeling pathetic and in shame for my weakness.

I always ended up being the dramatic one you know the crying drunk one begging them not to leave me, I can't live without you I promise I won't do anything to upset you again.

Some men feed off that feeding their ego and pride.

When we give our vulnerability to the wrong person they can harm our whole being. Make you more insecure more isolated.

I was just in a relationship where my shine was too much for this man. Now I know it will take a Godly man to who can handle my energy and my shine.

Depression and anxiety were manifested in being in the wrong relationship with not knowing my worth and settling for second best or good enough.

It gives them more power and control because you put all your worth, low self-esteem, fear, insecurities and put it in a nice box with a big red bow on it and give it to them. We need to do that and leave it on the throne with Jesus. The almighty healer and comforter he knows your heart and all your struggles.

John 8:12

When Jesus spoke again to the people, he said 'I am the light of the world.

Whoever follows me will walk in darkness but will have the light of life!

I always felt so raw after, pathetic, desperate and ashamed of myself. I would try my hardest for weeks to pretend I was not dying inside because they were not the 'one'. Trying to get them to love me the way I needed, but where clueless and when you are unequally yoked more hardship comes from it.

I mean seriously we are not meant to heal and fix our partners that is Jesus job. Yes, we love unconditionally but again find a partner who loves Jesus and desires to know your love language if you pick wrong again and for all the wrong reasons you will be stuck in a destructive choice you made again.

Fear of being alone fear of not finding anyone else. Those fears kept me hostage for years, and I have to daily fight the strongholds in my mind to stay on my destiny.

Being an escort, I prayed daily for my safety and health. I did have a couple incidents where I got roughed up. Having a job that you have to worry about if you are going to get raped, killed and thrown over the balcony is tormenting. Thinking about my kids but feeling absolutely stuck. The second time being roughed up I went into survival mode. The man was into treating a woman like property telling me to call him master. When I refused he bit me and slapped me until I couldn't hear out of my left ear. I refused to call him my master in my heart even then I knew I only had one master Jesus Christ. I remember lying there looking up at the ceiling and thinking God this is what you allow to happen to me????

Then I saw a vision Jesus shone his presence on me, and I saw his tears and compassion for me. It hurt Him more to see his daughter treated this way and being stuck in slavery.

And the time God delivered me from a client I always blocked a client after seeing him, if they treated me disrespectfully or were too rough. One day I went to answer the door and there standing in front of me was a man I had seen a couple times before. He had shared with me how he was gang affiliated and he just got out of jail now. I have my fair share of tattoos but this man was totally covered face to feet I could just see his eyes and mouth through it all…. It frightened me to just be in his presence. But I was also intimidated by him, I had blocked him because his aggression was growing with each session. Last time holding my face down on the bed so I couldn't breathe. Calling me the most horrible names like a dirty whore, slut… each minute I was with him I felt my self-worth being torn from me, each word he said, each time he tossed me around for his pleasure like a rag doll. Again, I went into survival mode he slapped my face continually. The last time I had seen him I was out of working for a week to heal from the bruises he left on me and the fear he put in me to see new clients.

You can imagine my heartache when I opened the door and it was him. He used a different number and pretended to be someone else he pushed past me saying hey beautiful I have missed you.

I felt sick I sat him down in the living room and excused myself to use the washroom. As soon I closed the door I fell to my knees and prayed to God please Lord I cannot go through that again he will break me. I pulled myself together wiped my tears away and returned to the living room. Upon my arrival, he stood up with his phone in his hand and said I got to leave, just got an emergency call. Again, when he left and I closed the door I fell to my knees in gratitude.

If you struggle knowing your worth perhaps this will help you as it had done for me.

To try and live daily in a servant attitude, wake up daily to live not for yourself but for the cause of Christ.

Ephesians 6:7

Serve wholeheartedly, as if you were serving the Lord, not men.

"People grow when they are loved well if you want to help others heal, love them without an agenda.

Because you know that the Lord will reward everyone for whoever does good he does whether he is slave or free!

Ever notice the joy and peace we get when we do something nice for someone? Blessing others is the best defence for depression it gets your mind off of it! "The habits you created to survive will no longer serve you when it's time to thrive.

Get out of survival mode. New habits, new life.

Ebonee Davis

> "Grief, I've learned is really just love.
> It's all the love you want to give but cannot.
> All that unspent love gathers up in the corner
>   of your eyes
> The lump in your throat, and in that hollow part
>   of your chest
> Grief is just love with no place to go
> Jamie Anderson

I have to wake up daily and before I start my day I give it all to Jesus his will be done in my life, and to give me strength and courage to fight the good fight of faith.

And when I don't I get lost in the battle of this world, left weak-willed blowing wherever the wind is. I go to Him and I be still.

Jesus is also showing me the power of tears when you cry you let out all the grief.

He showed me it is not weakness, it's God's given way to release the grief. Allow yourself to be vulnerable and after a while, you will welcome the cry. There were times when I would be left exhausted for days after eyes swollen totally drained. Roots pulled out of me so deep it was painful.

Because with it you get cleaned, washed away cleaner exhausted yes but you get back up and get back on your path your destiny.

Parents allow your children to be vulnerable and to cry, God designed us this way no shame just healing.

Sometimes when we wake up to spirituality, and you've seen it everywhere, the -you-know-what hits the fan. And everything falls apart. Those are the moments we get to work.

Those are not the moments when we drink. Those are not the moments when we go back to addiction. Those are the moments when we get to work.

Because those moments are showing up to help you show up. Pay attention to the assignments that are coming to you!

Everything comes up so it can be healed.

Gabrielle Bernstein

One of my biggest challenges right now is having to be on my own, having to remind myself what I am leaving behind is so worth the cost.

The Lord has given me visions of my future husband, not his face but his character a man after God's heart. He is full of life and encouragement and lifts me up as I do for him, and one day I finally will meet a man who respects and honours God first then me.

I always felt the lack when I was in these wrong relationships. God does not want me to beg for attention, God never makes us beg Him for attention.

But the flesh wants what the flesh wants. And the longer we keep living one foot in the grave and one foot out in the world the longer we stay in purgatory meanings = any condition or place of temporary punishment, suffering, expiation, or the like.

Serving to cleanse, purify or expiate.

Expiate means to atone for, make amends for, make up for, do penance for, pay for, redress, redeem, offset, make good "the desire to expiate his sins"

Now hear this yes, we know our sins are forgiven for Christ died for our sins but we have to daily die to our flesh and when you don't?

2 Peter 2:15

They have left the straight way and wandered off to follow the way of Balaam son of Beor, who loved wages of wickedness. But he was rebuked for his wrongdoings by a donkey a beast without speech who spoke with a man's voice and restrained the prophet's madness.

These men are like springs without water and mists driven by a storm. Blackest darkness is reserved for them. For they mouth empty, boastful words and by appealing to the lustful desires of sinful nature, they entice people who are just escaping from those who live in error.

They promise freedom while they themselves are slaves of depravity, for a man is a slave to whatever he has mastered. If they have escaped the corruption of the world by knowing our Lord and Savior Jesus Christ and are again tangled in it and overcome, they are worse off at the end then they were at the beginning.

Just as we who are parents have the responsibility to raise and teach our children. Our heavenly father is waiting for our hearts wide open, humble teachable spirits so he can mould us in his glory.

One thing I have learned is that when you try to numb yourself out with drugs, booze, sex whatever your vice is, when you are numbing yourself out, you disconnect yourself from God.

When you are so drunk your blackout, you disconnect from God.

Our bodies are a temple of God when you are poisoning it with drugs or booze or too much food, we are still living in the flesh.

And when that urge kicks in you are in a battle between good and evil. Being high I could not connect with God or anyone else. And it's tormenting you can't calm your mind and my thoughts were always dark., lonely, tormenting.

You become paranoid and act on that paranoia isolate yourself because you know people will know they will see you are high. Checking the windows seeing if anyone is there. Focusing on every bad thing that has ever happened to you! After thinking this is supposed to be my tap out

But really, I am in hell with no control over anything!

Being in bondage to addictions of any sort is such a tormenting death.

Now when you are in addiction and sin, you can't see it till you come out of it here is what God says Proverbs 26:4- 7 Do not answer a fool according to his folly, or you will be like him yourself.

Answer a fool according to his folly, or he will be wise in his own eyes.

Like cutting off one's feet or drinking, or violence is the sending message by the hand of a fool.

Proverbs 26:11 As a dog returns to his vomit, so a fool repeats his folly.

There are several types of fools referred to in this book of Proverbs, from the naive or simple-minded to the shameless and contemptible. The fool referred to in these verses is one who is obtuse, insensible and even averse to the truth. Such people must be controlled by force, like dumb animals. They can't be reasoned with or trusted, wisdom is useless to them, and honour is wasted on them. They are likely to be know it all, high on their own lists but low on everyone else's. They don't learn from their mistakes but repeat them over and over. Fools who read these verses will deny they have a problem, therefore the wisdom here is for those who must live with a fool. In order to operate wisely in relationships, we need to know with whom we are dealing with and act accordingly.

I was and surrounded myself with fools when I wanted to leave Jesus behind, and go out and party and dance the night away. Just escape all the pressures in my life.

Galatians 5:16-26

Live by the Spirit

So, I say, live by the spirit, and you will not gratify the desires of the sinful nature. For the sinful nature desires what is contrary to the Spirit, and the Spirit what is contrary to the sinful nature.

They are in conflict with each other so that you do not do what you want. But if you are led by the Spirit, you are not under acts of the law.

The acts of the sinful nature are obvious, sexual immorality, impurity and debauchery, idolatry and witchcraft, hatred, discord, jealousy, fits of rage, self-ambition, dissensions, factions and envy, drunkenness, orgies, and the like. I warn you, as I did before those of you who live life like this will not inherit the kingdom of God.

But the fruit of the spirit is love, joy, peace, patience, kindness, goodness, faithfulness, gentleness and self-control. Against such things, there is no law. Those who belong to Christ Jesus have crucified the sinful nature with its passions and desires. Since we live by the spirit, let us keep in step with the Spirit. Let us not become conceited, provoking and envying each other.

I was swallowed up in my sinful nature, going to sex houses where it was filled with lusts, desires and drugs and booze.

I always felt like I left my soul at the door when I entered those places thinking God is not here, he would not come into this filth but he was there with me even though I was lost in sexual immorality, impurity and debauchery, idolatry, hatred, discord, jealousy, fits of rage, self-ambition, factions and envy, drunkenness, orgies, drugs.

If I allowed myself to listen to the lies the enemy told me all that I was not, I would never have seen my self-worth through the eyes of the Son of God.

Towards the end of my lifestyle living in that hell, I started to realize God is with us in everything once we give Him our life which I had twenty- three years ago. But eight years ago, I became his prodigal daughter, but like I shared before, God will use you to reach the lost if you allow Him too. I would be in these bathhouses (sex houses) and Holy Spirit still spoke to me I would see people having unprotected sex with strangers and I would say to them it only takes once for you to get an S.T.D or worse H.I.V, or Hepatitis C. It brings me such peace knowing I will never put myself in those places again under those circumstances.

Galatians 6:1-5

Doing Good to All

Brothers, if someone is caught in a sin, you who are spiritual should restore him gently. But watch yourself, or you also may be tempted. Carry each other's burdens, and in this way, you will fulfill the law of Christ. If anyone thinks he is something when he is nothing, deceives himself. Each one should test his own actions. Then he can pride in himself, without comparing himself to somebody else, for each one should carry our own load.

My whole life I wish I could have wished to have someone carry my emotional load for me, that's my downfall, but there is no growth in that, we will not become dependent on God until we choose to.

Taking responsibility for our unforgiveness in others is so freeing, that is when The Holy Spirit showed me where my rage came from. Trying to hold others who have wronged me accountable.

Then when I choose to be still, Holy Spirit showed me every person I held responsible for my anger and bitterness every single person I felt wronged me ....

My Ma He showed me her upbringing full of abuse and insecurities. He showed me her love for me, how she was raised in a Catholic convict her young years, the abuse that happened in those places is unspeakable and leave scars only the healer can heal. Once I understood it had nothing to do with me, she loved me and she did her best with what she knew. All the anger I had was replaced with love and understanding. I talked on the phone with her for an hour right after, I still walk in forgiveness for her and love her! She has become one of my best encouragers with this book!

My ex-husband my eyes opened to see and understand all the abuse he endured as a child, he loved me the only way he knew how. Letting go of all bitterness of not feeling like he helped me raise our children. Being able to let go of all the things I thought he owed me.

My ex-boyfriend who I detoxed on my couch for fourteen days of oxycodone bringing him to church. He gave his life to Christ but choose to go back to his old lifestyle, again it had nothing to do with my worth why it didn't work out. I released all the bitterness with understanding.

My ex-boyfriend who I met being an escort he was a Christian man, he showed me how it was like to be treated like by a gentleman. He brought out the lady in me polished off my rough edges, led me into the desire to get out of prostitution. Confirming God did not want this life I was living. He went back to his family after attending church with me and I respected his choice. I finally got out of slavery three years later. God is good Amen!

Once we take ourselves out of the offence and ask Holy Spirit to show us where the root of unforgiveness is hiding, and where bitterness has taken root, stand firm in faith have your heart wide open be still in God and watch Him do his thing!

God showed me one evening just being still in His presence how by my own selfish desire, I was hurting these men. I was trying to cling on so tightly, I knew in my heart they were not my destiny and I would come to the realization of it and break it off with them. Then get lonely and beg them to come back.

I would use all my charm and manipulation to lure them back. Possibly putting bitterness in their heart, I don't want to ever be responsible for anyone's heartache.

My prayer and hope are that you get encouragement from this book, that you see all of God's goodness and that no matter where you are in life right now. It's never too late, you are not a lost cause!

So, wait on God even when you feel like your time has run up…. It's in these moments that our faith manifests, gets stronger. It's in these moments in total obedience that God says YES!!!! He then has full authority to work his glory, nothing pleases Him more than when we totally trust Him and give Him all our sins so we can be forgiven.

Nothing like total obedience to the Highest then the enemy is defeated against any assignment against you!

I don't regret any of the choices I have made, I have made my peace with them and know I am forgiven.

Do I sometimes wonder where I would be if I would have waited on the Lord? Yes, but I don't allow myself to stay there, would there have been less heartache I believe so. But I would not change my journey if it helps even one person, gives them hope to keep fighting the good fight of faith! It is well with me... Amelia Rose

Breaking the Rebellious Spirit

The Armor of God

Finally, be strong in the Lord and all his mighty power. Put on the full armour of God so that you can take your stand against the devil's schemes.

For your struggles is not against flesh and blood, but against the rulers, against the authorities, against the powers of this dark world and against the spiritual forces of the evil in the heavenly realms.

Therefore, put on the full armour of God, so that when the day of evil comes, you may be able to stand your ground, and after you have done everything, to stand.

Stand firm then, with the belt of truth buckled around your waist, with the breastplate of righteousness in place, and with your feet fitted with the readiness that comes from the Gospel of peace.

In addition to all this, take up the shield of faith with which you can extinguish all the flaming arrows of the evil one.

Take the helmet of salvation and the sword of the Spirit, which is the word of God. And pray in the Spirit on all occasions with all kinds of prayers and requests.With this in mind, be alert and always keep on praying for all the Saints.

Pray for me also that whenever I open my mouth, words may be given me so I will fearlessly make known the mystery of the Gospel, for which I am an ambassador in chains.

Pray that I may declare it as fearlessly as I should.

I never fully understood this verse until I started practicing it daily, I have a friend who is a professional bodybuilder. I started to train with her to get my body in optimal health and let me tell you of the commitment it takes to live that lifestyle. Controlled healthy eating, the weekly workouts the dying to what the flesh desires.

The battle starts in our minds to have victory over the temptation to sin. Just as a professional athlete trains their body and mind to come into agreement of their passion for their sport.

Dying daily to temptation and no motivation they "will' their minds and body to conform to its new blueprint.

We need to stand firm in God's truth and promises fight the good fight of faith so we can put out all the lies of the enemy.

Stay alert with our minds, stay aware of the schemes of the enemy, pray steadfastly.

Pray Holy Spirit's fearless love that you may go out boldly into the world and make known the Gospel to bring home all his rebellious children.

Amen.

Breaking the Rebellious Spirit

Praise Him

> Psalm 34:1 His praise will always be on my lips.
> Psalm 105:5 Sing to Him, praise Him.
> Mathew 5:16 And praise your father in heaven.
> Hebrew 13:15 Offer God a sacrifice of praise.

Learning to praise our Lord when we are our weakest is the key to breaking the lies of the enemy the torment stops. I know for myself when I get lost and am blowing in whichever way the wind is blowing.

When I plant my feet firmly in the Holy Spirit he is my compass he is my life teacher worthy of all the praise and glory.

I have been learning to praise Him daily throughout the day, in every moment the good the bad He wants it all.

When I am being attacked or when my spirit feels uneasy, I put on praise and worship music and start lifting my hands to Him, thanking Him for all the things He is doing in my life and for all the good that is yet to come.

It's sometimes the hardest to praise Him in the darkness of hopelessness, anxiety or depression is having dominion over you, and you don't have an ounce of energy left in you. Give whatever you have left in you give it all to Jesus

He is the only solution he can and will calm any storm.

1 Peter 4:11

If anyone speaks, he should do it as one speaking the very words of God.

If anyone serves, he should do it with the strength God provides, so that in all things God may be praised through Jesus Christ.

To Him be the glory and power forever and ever Amen

God wants all of us the good, the rebellion and all the ugliness in us, the addictions, the oppression the disobedience.

When we wholeheartedly praise Him even in our darkest times, we are showing God we believe even if our hearts are not able to at that moment. What happens is Holy Spirit comes in binds us back up, making us stronger and humble through his love for us and his grace and mercy for us.

Don't allow the enemy to come in with his lies, never have shame in praising God

Ask Holy Spirit to give you a heart that wholeheartedly yearns to praise Him., to fill you with the desire to present yourself before Him all your flaws all your insecurities all your doubts and pray that your heart bursts open to Him and all His truths.

Amen

Breaking the Rebellious Spirit

Keeping Faith

Hebrews 13:8

Jesus Christ is the same yesterday and today and forever.

Jesus never changes period.

People have disappointed us over and over throughout our lives, and even more so if we have had abusive relationships that have brought deep wounds and damaged us.

Keeping faith has meant to me …. In those moments of white knuckling it, when your back is pushed hard against that mountain or wall. Faith means you don't give up, you don't give in!

When the time has run up for that miracle you were believing. That is when you need to kick into high gear your faith. That is when the enemy is at his sneakiest his goal is to keep us in bondage to his lies, he attacks your mind trying to convince you, you are not worth the miracle you seek.

That's exactly when you stand on the promises of God with every lie that the enemy attacks with, replace it with his truth and promises.

You give your faith to a doctor when you break an arm and he fixes you up, puts a cast on you, tells you in 6-8 weeks it will be healed. You go about your next week's not in fear that it won't be healed.

Faith is believing in something that hasn't manifested itself yet. Faith is believing in something that you can't control.

Faith is believing in something that is going to happen, but it hasn't yet.

Mathew 9:29

Then he touched their eyes and said: "according to your faith it will be done".

Are you lost in the lies you can't beat this addiction, you will never get out of debt, you will never find that partner you want so badly?

Romans 10:17

Consequently, faith comes from hearing the message, and the message is heard through the word of Christ.

Pray that Holy Spirit gives you a steadfast faith that comes from hearing the Word. And when your faith is tested that you will go to the word for truth and the truth will set you free!

Amen

Breaking the Rebellious Spirit

Slaves and masters

Mathew 6:22-24

The eye is the lamp of the body. If your eyes are good, your whole body will be full of light. But if your eyes are bad, your whole body will be full of darkness. If then the light within you is darkness, how great the darkness.

No one can serve two masters. Either he will hate the one and love the other, or he will be devoted to one and despise the other. You cannot serve both God and Money.

Pray for Jesus to make your eyes good, eyes that are open to all his truth!

Pray that your deepest desire is to serve only one God... The almighty God in heaven. Amen!

Ephesians 5-8

Slaves, obey your earthly masters with respect and fear, and sincerity of heart, just as you would obey Christ. Obey them not only to win their favour when their eye is on you but like slaves of Christ, doing the will of God from your heart. Serve wholeheartedly, as is you were serving the Lord, not men because we know that the Lord will reward everyone for whatever good he does, whether he is slave or free.

Pray that God gives you a servant heart, a heart that is sincere in everything you do.

Pray God gives you an obedient heart one that hungers for all his truth all his goodness and done in all his love always. Amen!

God had to break my pride and my bitterness, I had in me. My issue of not wanting to be obedient to always want things my way, despising any type of authority pushing against me.

He had to replace it with a servant heart that was quick to forgive, humble to repent and full of love for his people with a love that only is obtained by serving the only true master, Jesus Christ!

Breaking the Rebellious Spirit

Be still and know He is God

Psalm 46

God is our refuge and strength, an ever-present help in trouble. Therefore, we will not fear, though the earth give way the earth give way, and mountains fall into the heart of the sea, though its waters roar and foam and mountains quake with their surging.

There is a river whose streams make glad the city of God, the holy place where the Highest dwells. God is within her, she will not fail, God will help her at break of day.

Nations are in uproar, kingdoms fall, he lifts his voice, the earth melts. The Lord Almighty is with us, and Jacob is our fortress.

Come and see the works of the Lord, the desolations he has brought on the earth. He makes wars cease to the ends of the earth, he breaks the bow and shatters the spear, he burns the shields with fire.

Be still and know that I am God. I will be exalted among nations, I will Almighty be with us, the Lord is our fortress.

The biggest revelation is this verse when I started on this journey as his rebellious daughter. Were my anger and fear was coming from not being able to trust anyone, I didn't even trust myself.

I had to learn to trust God my life was a complete mess before he came in and cleaned up the house, the more I gave Him, the more I trusted Him, the more obedient I became. When I would get lost in my old ways, old habits, He would whisper "Be Still and know I am God" I would calm my mind take some deep breaths and say okay Lord I trust you. The more I did this the more revelations and blessings came into my life.

Now when I get that uneasy feeling or I feel my anxiety brimming, or the attacks from the enemy are fierce. I go and be still with God to his peace, to his love he's my refuge, and when I am Still with Him is when he guides me shows me my next move. When I am still I can hear his voice bask in his presence, my rebellion dies at his feet.

Pray, God brings a deep desire in me to want to be "Still and know you are God. Bring light and deliver me of any roots of rebellion still in me. Replace them with roots of trust and obedience in you that grow so deep into my heart they can never be pulled out.

Amen

Breaking the Rebellious Spirit

Courage

1 Corinthians 16:13

Be on guard, stand firm in the faith, be men of courage, be strong. Do everything in love.

Deuteronomy 31:6-8

Be strong and courageous. Do not be afraid or terrified because of them, for the Lord your God goes with you, he will never leave you or forsake you.

Then Moses summoned Joshua and said to him in the presence of all Israel, be strong and courageous, for you must go with this people into the land that the Lord swore to their forefathers to give them, and you must divide it among them as their inheritance. The Lord Himself goes before you and will be with you, he will never leave you and forsake you. Do not be afraid, do not be discouraged.

Joshua 1:6-9

Be strong and courageous, because you will lead these people to inherit the land I swore to their forefathers to give them. Be strong and very courageous. Be careful to obey all the law my Servant Moses gave you, do not turn from it to the right or left, that you may be successful wherever you go. Do not let this Book of Law depart from your mouth, meditate on it day and night, so that you may be careful to do everything written in it. Then you will be prosperous and successful. Have I not commanded you? Be strong and courageous. Do not be terrified, do not be discouraged, for the Lord your God will be with you wherever you go.

When I started praying for Holy Spirit to give me a courage that surpasses all my understanding, when terror would try and rise in me I looked back on all the battles I've been victorious in and meditated on his promises in these verses.

A peace and fierceness would rise in me, being able to depend on his truth and his promises that he goes ahead of us in each battle, that you can be assured that he will never leave us or forsake us.

Pray Holy Spirit I ask that you rise up in me whenever any fear, or battle I need to arises, instill a courage in me to do all that you ask of me, instill in me a heart eager to obey you.

The deepest desire to meditate on your word so I can be victorious in all things.

Amen!

Breaking the Rebellious Spirit

Strength

2 Samuel 22:31-33

As for God, his way is perfect, the word of the Lord is flawless. He is a shield for all who take refuge in Him.

For who is God besides the Lord? And who is the rock except our God?

It is God who arms me with strength and makes my way perfect.

47-50

The Lord lives! Praise be to my Rock! Exalted be God, the Rock, my Savior!

He is the God who avenges me, who puts the nations under me, who sets me free from my enemies.

You exalted me above my foes, from violent men you rescued me.

Therefore, I will praise you. O Lord, among nations, I will sing praises to your name.

I have witnessed in my own life God's strength on rescuing me from violent men. Rescuing me from myself, rescuing me from situations my rebellion took me.

Giving me a strength that only comes from Him, a strength that makes me push on…. I can't turn back he has brought me so far, I live in His presence.

Pray God ingrain in me your strength so deep are the roots, they can never be pulled out, and be my rock and run to you when I need strength. Amen

Rise up! Fight your fight to freedom in Christ!

Amelia Rose